Wellness Manual

LEONA SOKOLOVA

PAGE PUBLISHING, INC.
Conneaut Lake, PA

First originally published by Page Publishing 2021

ISBN 978-1-6624-2726-8 (pbk)
ISBN 978-1-6624-2727-5 (digital)

Printed in the United States of America

Contents

*Just like the lotus, we too have the ability
to rise from the mud, bloom out of the
darkness, and radiate into the world.*
—Unknown

*The lotus is the most beautiful flower,
whose petals open one by one. But it will
only grow in the mud. In order to grow
and gain wisdom, first you must have
the mud—the obstacles of life and its
suffering... The mud speaks of the common
ground that humans share, no matter
what our stations in life... Whether we
have it all or we have nothing, we are all
faced with the same obstacles: sadness, loss,
illness, dying, and death. If we are to strive
as human beings to gain more wisdom,
more kindness, and more compassion,
we must have the intention to grow as a
lotus and open each petal one by one.*
—Goldie Hawn

The lotus flower symbolizes renewal, transformation, and new beginnings. It's also my favorite flower.

Dedication

To two extraordinary women: my incredible and beautiful mother, Leona, and my wise and compassionate grandmother Paulina who I love so much. They taught me well, and I am very grateful for their loving support.

Acknowledgments

I'd like to express my deepest gratitude to the talented people who contributed their time, energy, and love to this book. I've had a fantastic time working with each of them.

Paulina Korkuz is an excellent English teacher. She is conscientious, cordial and she lovingly offered her skillful help in creating a book cover design. I greatly appreciate her artistic vision in formatting and editing as well.

David Warshawsky is my dear friend. His editorial notes and his constructive criticism encouraged me to do my best. He reads a lot and has a keen eye for details.

Anatoly Ryvkin, who took the photos in this book, is a professional photographer, videographer, and web designer who does astonishing work.

Catherine Martinez is my lovely assistant. She is kind and positive and has helped me a great deal, in the process of writing my book, with her technological skills. I've taken pleasure in working with her.

A special thanks to Page Publishing and their publication coordinator Trevor Boyd, along with his publication team. They have done marvelous work in getting my book published.

All these people are skilled in different ways. I'm extremely grateful for their generous support and assistance. They are extraordinarily talented in their fields.

These wonderful people have read the manuscript of this book. I like different people's perspectives on my writing to make it perfectly polished. Their comments and observations are helpful and very necessary. I've addressed all their suggestions to improve this book and make it as refined, simple, and interesting as possible.

My Philosophy

People should be beautiful in every way—
in their faces, in the way they dress, in their
thoughts, and in their innermost selves.
                              —Anton Chekhov

I take pleasure in sharing with you the idea that being happy and healthy can be easy and incredibly rewarding. I'm very familiar with and in love with everything that wellness involves. My approach to wellness is simple. If you want to be at your best, just learn to pay close attention to these very important areas: thinking positively, having goals, eating well, drinking healthy beverages, and exercising regularly. When you focus on these, your health will respond. My own philosophy is that health, beauty, energy, and peace of mind come only when the body, mind, and spirit are in balance. We can bring out our inner vitality through positive attitudes, self-love, proper nutrition, and adequate exercise, rest, and relaxation.

I'd like to share with you radiant health, enjoyable nutrition, and a lovable lifestyle. I have a passion for these subjects. I've created my own unique method of exploring life and myself. My perceptions, life experiences, and love affair with feeling good have translated into this book.

My goal is to help people eat well, feel great at any age and see life positively. I always look for opportunities to inspire others to bring out the best in themselves.

I believe in the order of the universe. Whatever happens guides us toward healing, learning, and growth. I also believe in the Law of Attraction: happy attracts happy.

I look at life holistically. Holistic health involves the idea that everything in our lives affects everything else. I believe in simplicity, achievement, and moderation. I'm always trying to learn and grow in every way possible, and I want to encourage others to do the same and to choose inner balance and excellent health. I want to come into people's lives when they most need guidance and comfort, make a positive difference, share my passion for healthy living, and encourage them to choose the best, reach their health goals, enjoy day-to-day reality, and achieve an ideal lifestyle. The more quality attention we invest in our precious well-being, the more content and energetic we feel.

As you get acquainted with my philosophy, I'd like to invite you to consider some conscientious remarks that can be incorporated into your lifestyle. You'll be able to see for yourself how simple and enjoyable it is to lead a healthy and pleasant life.

I live by a wonderful saying: "You get what you send out." Do good things, and good things will come to you. I try to act according to my philosophy. I'm very excited to help and support you on your path to your best life. When you're at a point in your life where you don't know what to do or you're lost in terms of health, goals, and choices, embark on a journey of getting to know yourself and loving yourself more. This journey will guide you. The making of a special you and accepting yourself as you are, are extraordinary processes.

I believe in discovering what nourishes me and developing the best possible relationship with myself. I treat every aspect of my life with love, respect, and reverence. I live by my philosophy, and it feels great. Be good and kind to yourself and others.

A Search for Fulfilment

Many of us are searching for health, happiness, love, peace of mind, and balance. I understand that I'm responsible for my own development.

When life takes me through ups and downs—especially downs—I need to ease my emotional pain and focus on personal exploration. What I focus on expands.

I've become interested in exploring my spirituality. Some of the spiritual principles of self-enrichment that I turn to include the following:

- The importance of positive thoughts
- The importance of emotional balance
- The importance of gratitude
- The importance of forgiveness
- The importance of making peace with yourself
- The importance of enjoying the present moment
- The importance of simplicity
- The importance of love
- The importance of trusting
- The importance of proper nutrition, exercise, and breathing

This list is extensive, but I take one step at a time. These things help me reestablish the balance between my thoughts and my emotions.

The more I learn about spirituality, the more alluring it becomes. Exploring who I am is a long, exciting, and rewarding process. I gladly choose to spend time on self-introspection because it gradually crowds out emotional suffering. My personal enrichment is what I need in complicated life situations.

We are here on planet earth to learn and grow. So why don't we learn something valuable that stays with us forever and helps us achieve our best life and feel fulfilled?

Introduction

I'm one of many who go through life experiencing wonderful moments of comfort and joy and other moments of difficulty and sadness. I've lived through the challenges of searching for my calling and working on unfulfilling jobs. I've experienced lack of confidence, lack of self-love, procrastination, smoking, anemia, immigration, fears, divorce, and deception. To achieve balance, I've pursued my passions, self-exploration, self-enrichment, and spirituality.

We've all gone through similar challenging, happy, and hurtful events before we are ready to transform the way we live, the way we enjoy life, the way we think, the way we explore new territory, the way we perceive the beauty of everyday life, the way we love, and the way we see and imagine ourselves and others.

This is not my memoir. This is the story of how I've dealt with obstacles throughout my life. My intention is to promote change through a positive approach to life and to the difficulties life presents, and to help others enjoy day-to-day reality.

Life has many lessons to learn. Sometimes these lessons aren't realized until after the fact. My own sense of well-being and inner resilience have been deepened by the choices I've made when faced with challenging situations, not by the situations themselves. Everyone has a story of finding oneself. I want this book to contribute to your story, to your health, to your success, to your well-being, and to your balance.

This book is for everyone. Each person can relate to different topics and choose solutions to particular issues in their life or take away something to think about.

The *Wellness Manual* is really a guide through the process of introspection. The book is broken into sections, with tips on practicing positivity, gratitude, and love; eating well; exercising regularly; and more. It is about exploring and discovering what nourishes you in terms of mental and physical health. Mental health should be our primary concern; therefore, it's discussed first. Also, some people—myself included—need to prepare themselves mentally before acting. However, feel free to begin reading the "Physical Health" section first, if that appeals to you.

The majority of the ideas and suggestions in this book come from my personal experience and my own valuable insights that I gained from learning life lessons and the sources listed in the "Suggested Readings" section.

Each day, I learn more, and I always look forward to new discoveries. It's taken me more than thirty years to begin to understand and know myself. Perhaps you can benefit from my experiences and take a few shortcuts.

MENTAL HEALTH

CHAPTER 1

General Remarks about Misery

An old Cherokee told his grandson, "My son, there is a battle between two wolves inside us all. One is Evil. It is anger, greed, resentment, inferiority, lies, and ego. The other is Good. It is joy, peace, love, hope, humility, kindness, empathy, and truth."
The boy thought about it and asked, "Grandfather, which wolf wins?"
The old man quietly replied, "The one you feed."
—Cherokee Folktale

Sticky Misery

Misery creates a turbulent reality, while happiness creates a peaceful reality. Both of them crave our attention. It's a battle between misery and happiness. Which side wins? The winning side is the one that we pay close attention to, feed well, and choose to be our favorite. During this battle, we have the chance to explore our life story from an entirely new and unique perspective, discover our hidden selves, liberate ourselves from misery, develop a habit of looking for solutions that help us be healthy and happy, reflect on our lives, and see what we can improve to attain a more desirable reality. This can set the direction of our lives and determine our future. How can we be impervious to misery? How can we find joy on our life journey?

Let's analyze which reality is more appealing. Misery and stress equal stagnation, degradation, and a polluted mind. Misery produces much ugliness because it keeps us in negativity. Misery dictates negative actions, while our true needs go unattended. When we give misery, we receive misery. However, misery is not completely bad. It gives value to happiness, letting us see the contrast between the two. Without misery, we wouldn't appreciate what happiness feels like.

Happiness equals creativity, a healthy mind, abundance, and growth. Happiness is a feel-good emotion and can crowd out misery. Happiness produces absolute beauty and grace.

When people think negatively, they live in misery. When people think positively, they live in happiness. We can look at life from a dramatic point of view and feel miserable, or we can look at life from a lighthearted point of view and feel at ease. What's really important is to have something positive to believe. We can always choose positive over negative aspects of life or switch to a better subject—get off the subject that bothers us as soon as possible. We can clear the path for happiness and success with positivity. We can learn how to turn a destructive attitude into a constructive attitude and watch our dreams become reality.

The prevailing atmosphere is constant drama, fear, hurt, anger, insecurity, and death. All day, every day, we hear about murder and catastrophic events. Some of us think it's easier to live in stress and misery because it's so familiar. In the state of complete unawareness, when we go through each day without a good intention or agenda—feeling bored, having automatic behavior, or being grouchy—all kinds of negativity enter us easily. When we affirm the negative, we attract more of it. When we affirm something deeply and with conviction, it becomes real eventually. People remain in misery because they affirm misery.

People who are addicted to misery are against happiness. They delight in misfortune. When they listen to good news, they feel uncomfortable. When they encounter a happy person, they become angry and jealous of that person because they don't feel that sense of joy. A happy person emanates positive energy, which doesn't match their energy.

Ignorance and suffering have been spreading like cancer throughout each day. Social media have been feeding us ignorance and hugely imposing their points of view.

We've been listening to a ton of toxic stories. We're being miseducated by negative influences. We live in a culture that tells us that we should always live in fear. This decreases our happiness greatly, so we try to increase it through fighting back. That's why many people think life is a struggle.

The manifestations of ignorance include alcohol, over-ambition, drugs, negative comments, drama, discouraging news, laziness, depression, blame, envy, pride, judgment, jealousy, biases, vanity, greed, and criticism. I call these internal disturbers or inner clutter. All they do is take my attention away from positivity. They try to impose wrong and destructive beliefs. If I hold a wrong belief based on ignorance, it pollutes my mind with anger, worry, and discontent. Then I'm in misery. At times like this, it's good to look inward and see which reality I'm nourishing.

Misery attracts people's attention. When we're miserable, we feel special. We like being attended to and loved because of that. We crave this attention and feed off the energy of drama. People pity us, take care of us, comfort us, support our empty talk, discuss negative news of the day, and listen to and become miserable because of our gossip, complaints, and emotional minidramas.

We don't want to be alone with misery. We have a burning obsession to share it with our family, coworkers, friends, or even strangers. We want to infect others with our misery.

We're also very skillful at finding ways to criticize and blame. People even gather in groups and speak hatefully so that hate is multiplied to a very damaging degree. When we give hate, we receive hate. All the above don't benefit our lives at all.

There are many people around us who are attached to their misery. Everything they say is negative. Their grumpiness can affect us badly. They can inflict their bad mood on us. Every time I've had a draining and stressful conversation, I feel miserable because it sticks to me like dirt. But while dirt can be easily washed off, the toxicity of negative conversations doesn't come off as quickly. People emanate the negative energy of misery, and we pick it up. We mimic the people we spend time with, knowingly or unknowingly.

Misery and stress are like magnets that attract more misery and stress. And one day, we can be totally controlled and swallowed by them without even noticing. We become blinded by distasteful misery and stress. We get used to them easily, and they become automatic. Unfortunately, we are filled with complaints and excuses, and we choose this perception of our reality mechanically without realizing it, and we indulge in it.

Hopefully, once we finally wake up in the middle of sticky misery and unwanted ugly reality, we will know what to do—look at life from a positive perspective and try to live attentively and healthfully. There's one way to learn which way to go: educating ourselves. It's good to ask ourselves what we want so we can adopt good and useful information, sort it out, be selective with it, and use it to our advantage.

Have you ever longed to have the guts to leave the herd? I have. I used to smoke because everyone around me smoked. I was under the influence of the herd of smokers. One beautiful day, I faced this undesirable reality. I had an urge to smoke a cigarette in the morning. I pinched myself and said, "It's time to wake up, Darling, and quit smoking for my sake." It was destructive to my skin, teeth, and overall health. So I delivered myself from a horrible habit. I quit smoking easily and felt so good, happy, and relieved. I was free from a damaging influence and very proud of myself.

But quitting didn't happen out of the blue. The thought of quitting had been evolving in my mind for a while. It felt like I'd been waiting for the right moment when I'd be completely ready. During this process, I felt anger toward myself because one part of me wanted to smoke while another part wanted to be healthy. Eventually, I decided that to be wholesome is much more beneficial than to smoke and harm myself. I finally knew where the happiness button existed. It existed in my inner strength—a strong desire to be an individual and not copy others. This encouraged me to be willing to do the right thing and to become better. When I changed that habit, I felt awake and refreshed.

It seems we all have two buttons—a misery button and a happiness button. It's our choice which to activate. Do we want to mimic other people or develop the best version of ourselves? Do we want to blossom into a person of happiness and peace or stay the same?

If we had spent more time analyzing and correcting our indecisiveness and weaknesses, and less time creating excuses to defend them, we would now be in a better place. We would have understood that making excuses and alibis is fatal to our wellness.

When we realize our own power, it gives us a new perspective. We can stop blaming others and say to ourselves, "Whatever's happening, I'm responsible for my reaction to it, and I'm responsible for my actions, and I can change that reaction and those actions for the better."

We can always bring more positivity, emotional awareness, and kindness to our relationships with others and, more importantly, with ourselves.

My Story

Never complain, never explain,
resist the temptation to defend
yourself or make excuses.
—Brian Tracy

I had gone through a difficult divorce. I had been through the stress caused by that, as well as depression, blame, and judgment. When I was suffering from them, I had a conflict of which reality to choose. I was torn between the two worlds of misery and happiness. I was sure that my happiness and peace were buried under doubts, complaints, fear, indecisiveness, and worry. I was wired to gossip and rumors. I used to listen to people's negative stories about lack of health, money, time, energy, and love. I heard the same boring excuses again and again. I was hammered by them. I thought I was being respectful, but I was really just doing the same thing other people were. I tried to hide or justify my ignorance and misery with excuses. When I defended myself with them, I talked myself out of what I really wanted to do. Excuses stole my days, time, creativity, and energy.

It wasn't fun dragging myself from one day to the next and doing my activities mindlessly. I understood that I was under huge stress and misery and that they created a lot of suffering. Being stressed is widely acknowledged as a primary cause of many diseases, including depression. None of that is welcome in my precious life.

Misery is detrimental to good health, so I tried to steer away from it and become immune to it. There are two ways of life: to be ignorant about where I was and what I wanted to do and maybe go deeper into misery to the point of no return or to clean it up, bounce back from adversity, and discover peace of mind. I could continue complaining, or I could activate awareness, and when I would fall, I could get up, come to my senses, and move on with appreciation.

I was at a point in my life where I was ready to drop sticky misery for good and walk toward blissful peace and happiness. I was ready to disconnect from negativity and connect to positivity. I had to learn from these terrible experiences and build a happy feeling instead. As soon as I realized that, I transformed my thought patterns and beliefs to be free from the poison of misery and stress. The more I pondered, the clearer it was what I should be doing: liberating myself from them completely.

I could direct the energy of misery into doing something productive and channel the energy into a new project. It was a good opportunity to study something I'd never studied before. Learning new skills is admirable. There were many subjects I could choose from to refine myself and have a better quality of life. I had gone through the process of renewing myself and peeling off layers of misery and stress one by one to change my mentality to a fresh one—the mentality of a positive outlook. Change evolves gradually.

I knew there was a way to live my life differently and with more joy. I was determined to direct my undivided attention to filling myself and my life with happy thoughts and creative plans.

By reviewing my thoughts, activities, and the information that entered my mind, I could see clearly what benefited me. I could develop a true opinion of myself and others. I could give myself better entertainment than gossip. I could make my mood impervious to outer circumstances. In other words, I wondered what I could contribute to improve my life.

I was very serious about following the road of happiness and positivity. It was a perfect time to take a daily mental inventory. I promised myself I'd start that day—no more procrastinating.

I remember perfectly the day I began to embrace this challenge, to develop a healthier mindset, to develop a better perspective, and to start a happier life. I had an insatiable appetite for living in harmony with myself and others. I enjoyed every moment of this process.

During this period, I spent a lot of time alone and in silence, researching good ideas on how to live well. My first step was to explore and learn what made me happy and peaceful. I wrote down a list of activities that made me feel positive and uplifted. This was a beautiful time of personal enrichment. It became a happiness pact with myself and a quest that I loved, and I participated in it with real passion and enthusiasm, searching for the true treasure of my inner peace. It had been an exciting and empowering adventure, and a reliable method for getting where I wanted to go.

I was carefully creating a safe environment in which I felt comfortable. I was eager to leave misery behind and enter a realm of pure happiness, find balance and contentment, and manage to stay there indefinitely. I was ready to see truth and wisdom, and have the courage to be honest with myself. Being honest with myself, being unbiased and looking correctly, seeing things as they were, and maintaining a positive attitude helped me let go of suffering and move forward.

Once I had my fill of misery and stress, I stopped being bitter about my divorce. I was determined to make my life fruitful by creating a healthy lifestyle and valuing my peace and happiness. I was also determined to be less influenced by what others thought. If they said negative things, I didn't want to listen. But if they said encouraging things, I was happy to hear them.

The words we say to each other really matter. When I interact with other people, I try to swap information to inspire and support us all, speak loving words, focus on appreciation, spread good news and happy stories, spend time in a more interesting and enjoyable way, and be surrounded by people with similar agenda and interests. I also talk about how to improve health and wellness, attain peace of mind, find a lovely hobby, and think well about myself and others. The more I go in this direction, the less things upset me and the calmer and more nonreactive I become. Every single day, I can do better and better. Misery has gradually stepped back, and a friendlier reality has stepped forward.

Removing misery can be difficult, but it's possible. My approach is to look for peace and happiness. When I look at the positive side of life, examine where I am, and become more mindful, I will choose a better direction for my future, and I will find a way to rejoice.

Weighing the pros and cons of misery and happiness can help us make wise decisions. The way we use our beliefs, thoughts, words, and images affects our choices and helps us make a smooth transition to a happier life. What we encourage—misery or happiness—is what we obtain. It's our choice. We get what we choose. The decision should be fairly easy because the right choice always feels better.

I've learned a lot of things the hard way and can say that changes are challenging at first, confusing in the middle, and very rewarding at the end. Once I understand that happiness is something I design for the present moment and that it's a beautiful lifelong journey of learning to be more mindful in daily life, then I know how to attain long-term happiness.

I've challenged myself to use mindful living to crowd out stress and misery. Mindful living is a good way to enjoy living in the world without being affected by stress and to find happiness and peace, and create a strong relationship with them.

Mindful Living

Mindfulness is the energy of being aware and awake to the present moment. It is the continuous practice of touching life deeply in every moment of daily life. To be mindful is to be truly alive, present, and at one with those around you and with what you are doing. Through mindfulness, we can learn to live in the present moment instead of in the past and the future. Dwelling in the present moment is the only way to truly develop peace, both in one's self and in the world.
—Tich Nhat Hanh

I try to reflect on these wonderful words of wisdom and on being more mindful throughout each day.

When I'm surrounded with the beautiful energy of mindfulness and stillness, everything is peaceful and everything is lovely. I'm relaxed. I feel good, and I like that. There's no need to spoil my present enjoyment of life with thoughts and worries about the past and future. Nothing is worth more than being here and now, in the present. I love being in the moment of feeling good. It's a sweet spot to be in.

Here is my proposition. Just for a minute, shift your perspective and envision your life this day more slowly, with plenty of time for the things that matter most. Picture yourself poised and serene. Imagine that emotional and spiritual well-being is your top priority. Just align your attention to that. An immediate result of mindfulness is feeling calmer. It's worthwhile appreciating life's precious moments.

Mindful living is the key to peace and happiness. It can help us cultivate awareness of the beauty of the present moment. It can help us get in touch with our inner selves and quietness. It can also open the doors to our deepest needs and desires. Being mindful and joyful can be attained with ease and comfort.

The fantastic benefits of mindfulness include the following:

- Better support for good health and resilience
- Reduced stress
- Calmed mind
- Improved sleep

- Less reactivity and judgment
- Better decision-making
- More productivity in daily life
- Boosted mental clarity
- Diminished feelings of loneliness
- Better mood
- Better awareness of thoughts and feelings
- Healthier eating
- More motivation to exercise
- Increased curiosity about life

Being mindful means taking responsibility for what we say, think, and do. Being mindful is the foundation for happiness.

When I was introduced to the idea of mindful living, I applied it to my life. Now, I do my best to focus moment to moment and be present with myself. I try to do my daily activities mindfully, one thing at a time. I do this whenever I remember. I don't push it. I just enjoy it. It improves my mood quickly and benefits my well-being with lasting positive results.

As I become more mindful, a new reality becomes my lifestyle. For example, when I encounter an unpleasant situation, I pause and observe rather than react negatively. This makes me eager to interact with others, and I also feel better about myself. I make wiser choices throughout the day when it comes to how to eat, how to move, and how and where to take my breaks. It is especially helpful in situations where stress is high.

I've been thinking about mindful living a lot. It seems fun, peaceful, and calm. Living mindfully and joyfully is spirituality in action. Spirituality is transformative. We can always choose our style of spirituality. It can include mindful meditation, a gratitude journal, and communion with nature.

If we do this personal work of focusing on the present moment, we will be pleasantly surprised and rewarded with good health and peace of mind. We can live mindfully and feel fantastic every day.

Any activity—like taking a walk or cooking—can be done mindfully. One way to achieve mindfulness is meditation, which is a spiritual practice that can involve focusing on a particular thought or object or just listening to the sounds of nature.

Buddhists have been talking about and practicing meditation for centuries. Their style of meditation teaches us how to find peace and emotional calm. It isn't necessary to go on a retreat or to a monastery to learn to do it correctly, although it's a great idea to get meditation training from professionals. It's always available, and we can start mastering it right now. It just takes our willingness to believe in its benefits and to do it and to pay attention to the present moment. It's enjoyable and simple to practice.

We can start a practice at any age and do it in any environment. Many people turn to meditation to relieve stress and calm the mind. We can explore different styles of meditation and find one that's truly ours.

Meditation can also improve our mental health. Many people complain about being depressed or anxious. These are common health concerns. Depression can hit us when we brood on the past. Anxiety can visit us when we fret about the future. Mental health, balance, and peace of mind hug and comfort us when we stay in the present.

When we're in the present, there's nothing to fear or worry about. We can just be still and relish that moment. The peacefulness of the present moment erases anxiety and depression. Meditation is a natural therapy and can be helpful in treating both conditions. It can naturally restore a calm and peaceful state of mind to support health and happiness.

Other conditions can also benefit from meditation, but one should always consult a doctor first.

A Five-Minute Meditation

To the mind that is still, the whole universe surrenders.
—Lao Tzu

A few minutes of meditation are all we need to get centered. A few sets of one to five minutes throughout the day can help us gain a sense of calm. We pause, we breathe, and we savor this present moment. We pay undivided attention to each moment and to our sensations and thoughts. To be aware of the present moment, just say to yourself, "I'm here right now." Truly connect with yourself. Feel your whole body, feel your feet on the ground, and appreciate where you are.

Meditation must be done consistently for you to receive all its benefits. Once a day is good, but three times a day is optimal. Make it a friendly and pleasant routine.

Try these tips for a meditation session. Turn off your phone and put it away. Sit in a comfortable position and close your eyes. Be still and be present. Breathe in and breathe out, and only pay attention to your breathing. Or try to tenderly repeat a word or phrase or positive affirmation you like, or concentrate on a beautiful image. You can also count your breaths from one to ten and back to one. This will help you reach a calm state and lessen mental chatter. If your mind wanders, just bring it back. When you're done and relaxed, take your time and enjoy your day.

Have you truly listened to the sound of the sea? The other day, I sat on the rocks overlooking the ocean and really focused on the sound of the waves moving back and forth, and smelled the fresh and salty air. One way to beauty, true peace, and happiness is to savor peace and joy in the moment. This moment is our life. Being totally present feels exquisite. There's no better time to experience the sweetest present moment than NOW.

Have you thought about the fantastic benefits of mindfulness?

CHAPTER 2

General Remarks about Gratitude

Learn to be thankful for what you already have, while you pursue all that you want.
—Jim Rohn

The Gratitude Journal

Have you caught yourself ruminating over the negative lately? If your answer is yes, it's definitely a great time to start a gratitude journal. We have so many things to be grateful for. Why don't we live a life of gratitude? A sense of gratefulness can lead to radiant health and a pleasant mood. Feeling thankful for what we already have helps us achieve clarity about ourselves and our situations, whether they're good or far from ideal. Writing in a gratitude journal can be very helpful when we want to understand our emotional and physical self. Concentrate on who you are and feel good about who you are, and the rest will fall into place.

Feeling grateful is beneficial for us. Its benefits include better sleep, mood, balance, appreciation of ourselves and others, health, communication, intention, and goals. We can have more satisfaction with life and more optimism.

Expressive writing can help us organize our thoughts and emotions, cleanse the mind, and find meaning and joy in any life experience. It can also help us become healthier, happier, and more energetic.

Journaling works for me; others may prefer to share their gratitude with a friend via text, email, phone, or other means of communication. Gratitude is also a great topic for conversation with friends on a similar path. Talking about gratitude can direct any conversation to an interesting discussion and a more positive space. It always feels uplifting and healthy when we talk about something good. It takes minimal effort and gives maximal rewards.

When I'm journaling, I try to relax and put myself in a positive mood. I go at my own pace. I record everything I think and feel. Which thoughts and feelings make me comfortable or uncomfortable? What happened today? How did it make me feel?

Writing my thoughts down has many rewards. I describe my life in detail, understand it better, learn from it, and improve it. It's a huge help to get to know myself better. And if there's something I need to get off my chest, it does that too.

With all these rewards, I decided to commit to thirty days of journaling to find my own style of gratitude. I enjoyed this adventure. I have the power to form or change any habit if I set my mind to it. Developing a daily journaling habit was simple, fun, and interesting.

As I practice gratitude, I realize its good influence. I stop taking things for granted. I feel calmer and more grounded in the present moment. A gratitude journal helps me stay conscious of my actions and plan ahead, which is exciting and is making my life better and easier.

Gratitude definitely has a boomerang effect—the good vibes we emanate always come back to us. I truly believe in the saying "You get what you send out." With that in mind, this can be the perfect time for you to start a gratitude habit. Making small lifestyle changes that become habits can make a huge difference. For instance, having freshly squeezed carrot juice is super nutritious. Exercising regularly is invigorating. Developing gratitude is physically and emotionally beneficial.

My Story

*If you want things to be different, perhaps
the answer is to become different yourself.*
—Norman Vincent Peale

I remember a time when I was less grateful. I was preoccupied with complaints, burdens, deprivations, excuses, and gossip. Gratitude journaling taught me to use better vocabulary, emphasize my appreciation for life, see good fortune and beauty everywhere I go. Gradually, I was ruminating less and less on the negative, thanks to the process of developing a more positive and appreciative outlook.

I began to view everything and everyone I met with gratitude and respect. Every morning, I wrote down five to eight things that I was grateful for and reflected on them for a minute or longer. This made it easier to start the day with a smile. I started by being thankful for simple things, like good weather, a morning cup of coffee, healthy food, comfortable bedsheets, soft pillows, healthy herbal toothpaste, a refreshing shower, body wash with a nice and fresh scent, colorful towels, a cozy bathrobe, and people who had been good to me. I was especially grateful for good health. My list became longer and more specific as I practiced this wonderful and exciting technique.

As I traveled in my daily life, I met different people, and different situations arose. These were good opportunities to observe myself and my family, friends, and others. The moment I began to understand myself better, I also began to understand and appreciate other people better.

By learning other people's perceptions and opinions, I could see a good contrast between pessimists and optimists. Optimism and pessimism are thinking styles. They can be easily spotted. These styles can also be changed. What separates people who are optimistic from those who are pessimistic is how they interpret and process the circumstances of life. Some of my friends were pessimistic. They had a negative outlook. They taught me how not to be one of them. When they shared their opinions, they could discourage me and even kill my dreams. I decided to keep my dreams and plans to myself and protect my boundaries. I came up with a kind of protection for myself, saying, "I'm in a wonderful mood, and I intend to stay there."

Positive beliefs are related to optimism, which is intertwined with how we view ourselves and the world around us. Optimism is a sense of confidence about the future, expecting a positive outcome, which definitely leads to success. When optimists deal with difficulties in life, they're more likely to cope with them well.

According to the Law of Attraction, if we think optimistically, we attract more optimism and joy.

My optimistic friends had a positive outlook. They searched for the positive in every situation. They taught me how to do this, and it made me happier, which I liked. *How about being more optimistic, forming that astounding habit, and becoming an eternal optimist?* I asked myself. It was the right time to choose a side. Without hesitation, I chose the positive. At the same time, I understood that it took effort to be more aware of my thoughts and attitudes. I also understood that I was responsible for my perceptions and responses.

Some unpleasant situations will always occur, but I can decide how I want to respond to them. I can always choose a positive side of any situation and move in that direction. It's always my choice to either step into the negative and waste my precious time and energy, or step into the positive and learn to stay there indefinitely. There's a bright side to everything. I just need to be willing to see it.

It was very interesting to observe people's communication around me, and I was curious to distinguish between more grateful people and less grateful people, and see where I belonged. Even though I thought I was on the positive side, to my surprise, I had a tendency to be negative and pessimistic. I could see very clearly that the prevailing moods around me were also negative. People often use unpleasant vocabulary. Words have consequences. They're like small boomerangs. Every word we send out vibrates and comes back to us sooner or later.

From what I saw, it was obvious that less grateful people were preoccupied with complaints, excuses, disbeliefs, doubts, drama, negative news, and gossip. At that time, I was no different, but I had the will to be different.

After realizing that my language was like that of the less grateful people, I decided to change my way of speaking and used warmer, more encouraging words. I advised myself to consciously build more pleasant vocabulary. There are so many beautiful adjectives. Why not use them and play with them often? Now, I always remember that nothing is sweeter to hear than warm, lovely, and inspiring talk.

I turned my attention to speaking like more grateful people. More grateful people use a language that emphasizes travel, gifts, joy, abundance, fashion, wellness, and health.

They said, for example, "I'm so happy. I'm going to join a yoga class. I'm going to spend my time in a great and healthy way. It's a golden opportunity for me to enjoy and advance." Their intentions and words were positive and constructive.

I suddenly found myself looking forward to finding new things in life to be appreciative of. I enjoyed this technique as often as possible. After the thirty days were over, I didn't want to stop. Now, gratitude journaling is part of my routine. The gratitude journal is a great tool to discover my inner nature and make peace with it. I am able to speak to myself while sorting out issues, getting familiar with what I want, appreciating people in my life with an open mind, and analyzing my thoughts, only leaving me with inspirational ones. The time I've spent journaling has helped me become more grateful, positive, and forgiving. Gradually, feel-good emotions have crowded out negativity. I can turn a less grateful attitude into a more grateful and exclusively positive one.

My friends were taken aback when they heard my cheerful talk. Then they wanted to emulate me. Positivity is contagious. They asked me what I did and what my strategy was. And I answered proudly: It was my gratitude journal.

For me, gratitude is all about seeing good fortune everywhere and being grateful for it. Having gratitude equals having excellent health and abundance. It enhances happiness. I anticipate starting each day being grateful and kind. Gratitude brings magic. One magical day turns into a magical month and a magical year. It feels good to notice the beauty around me, to caress my eyes with it, and to fill my mind with gratitude and positivity.

Speaking of beauty, one day, I read an article about the power of color. No wonder the seven vibrant colors of the rainbow have always fascinated me. I believe colors can communicate with us, sending different messages and making us happier.

I love visiting a flower shop or looking at a beautiful window display. It's like an avalanche of bright colors that distracts me from a hectic day and feeds my soul with a new and pleasant scene. It works like a charm. It takes only a few minutes of color therapy, and I'm in a different world—the world of absolute beauty—and in a much better mood.

I have learned from the article that every color has unique benefits. For instance, red motivates and stimulates and gives us strength and support in pursuing our dreams.

It counteracts negative thinking. Red food can increase our vitality and stamina.

Every week, I give myself a different assignment. For instance, for one week, I try noticing the color red: a red purse someone is carrying, a red car someone is driving, red flowers, and red fruit and vegetables. I enjoy all the colors, but this particular week is all about red. I love to look at red and wear red, as if trying to absorb all the benefits of that particular color. When I do that, I feel better and have more energy. Simple things bring a lot of pleasure.

I will devote another week to noticing orange—the color of happiness, courage, and contentment. Orange is a natural antidepressant; it creates optimism and motivation. I can notice orange flowers, fruits, and vegetables. I also plan to include orange in my wardrobe. It's a bold move for me, but I can start with some accessories.

A great assignment is focusing on treating people with a lot of respect and looking for opportunities to express my appreciation to someone every day and being super specific. For example, "Thank you for walking my dog this week. Thank you for being such a helpful assistant. I'm so grateful for your work on remodeling my home." This approach works for me. It brings peace and enjoyment. When we're thankful, we exude good energy. People sense it and respond to it with positivity. Don't be surprised if the good vibes come back to you. Just welcome them. You can always be grateful in a way that makes sense to you.

A different assignment can be looking for beautiful photos or videos of kittens, puppies, and nature. You can also watch a romantic comedy or sports, history, travel, or the Discovery Channel. Anything works if it makes us smile. The more activities we savor, the more grateful we become. This technique occupies my mind so I don't pay attention to less important things. I take pleasure in exploring the wonders of the beautiful world we live in and walking blissfully with gratitude for each lovely day.

Without a doubt, an acquired habit of gratitude leads to a more enjoyable and fulfilled life. It can be easily attained with a thirty-day journaling experiment in more appreciative living. You can practice the habit of gratitude all day long. Feel thankful and be happier every day. Be pleased with what you do for yourself and others, and what puts you in a happy mood.

If you want health, be grateful for the health you have right now. If you wish to be happy, be grateful for everything that makes you happy now. Look for reasons to be joyous. Be positive regularly. Listen with deep attention to your mind and body. Recognize your individuality and learn more about your needs. Soon, you will know what drains or energizes you.

Try new things with pleasure. Bring novelty into your days and savor life with a spirit of joy and adventure. Health, happiness, gratitude, and positivity are within our reach, waiting to be revealed.

Philosophy Matters

Our life is shaped by our mind;
we become what we think.
—Buddha

The School of Practical Philosophy was a big part of my journaling, learning, and growing. It had a tremendously positive impact on my confidence. I absolutely loved the school's warm environment. I still feel its benefits.

An acquaintance introduced me to the school. It's been awhile since I attended, but I used to enjoy going there on Sundays. There were interesting lectures and a nice café and bookstore where I could interact with other people who also appreciated philosophy.

I think we need to consider philosophy now more than ever. Many philosophers and spiritual teachers have spoken about the power of gratitude and happiness. The great philosophers of the East and West teach that happiness is within each of us. So how do we tap into it? We discussed this and other essential questions that faced every human being. What type of life provides the greatest happiness? The answer also lies within us. We must figure it out for ourselves, but philosophy can definitely guide us to that answer.

I took an introductory course to try to learn more. There were topics to study, practices to implement, and handouts to review. The classes were inspiring. It was a very exciting process that led me to self-discovery and self-enrichment, as well as meeting and interacting with like-minded people. The course showed me how great and helpful philosophical ideas were. They worked in the past, are effective in the present, and will work in the future. They are timeless knowledge. I'm very grateful that I can learn these profound ideas and put them to practical use in my daily life.

When I read the notes from the class called "Why Study Philosophy?", I learned that when areas of life seem uncertain, the study of philosophy can provide clarity and direction, especially those areas we constantly struggle with. Philosophy is designed to help us become more alert, to raise our awareness of our thinking and actions, and to help us see things as they are. I also learned this profound quote from Socrates: "The unexamined life is not worth living."

Even though I gained some wisdom from the School of Practical Philosophy, I wasn't yet ready to act on it. The time was right for me a year later. I had a strong desire to reexamine my life and to investigate it thoroughly. Then I made gratitude part of my spiritual practice. I tried to replace my old way of thinking with a new way of thinking—an attitude change for the better, by being grateful and positive toward everything.

What you focus on is what you'll get. I believe we're spiritual beings in a material world. Each of us arrives on earth with a different agenda; I had an innate curiosity about mine.

Spirituality is a slow but astounding process. Gratitude has become my style of spirituality, my ally, and my companion; it escorts me everywhere I go and reveals more about my true nature. My spiritual quest continues in getting to know myself better and more deeply. I've also become more interested in other people and more sympathetic toward them.

Philosophy provides me with tools I can use and gives me a lot to think about. There are key points to study: What is wisdom? What are the qualities of the wise man and woman? How can we become more attentive in our lives?

One of the tools I have acquired is the following meditation:

A Buddhist Meditation on Forgiveness for Oneself and Others

> *From my heart, I forgive you for whatever you did, intentional or not.*
> *May you be happy, free of confusion, and understand yourself and the world.*
> *Please forgive me for whatever I did to you, intentional or unintentional. May we open our hearts and minds to meet in love and understanding.*

Forgiveness: A Fresh Start

> *True forgiveness is when you can say*
> *"Thank you for that experience."*
> —Oprah Winfrey

The beauty of self-introspection is that it leads us from one step to another and from one issue to another lovingly, gradually, and consistently. Wanting to cultivate more positivity in my life led me to the gratitude journal. That led me to the issue of forgiveness. It came to the surface because of my gratitude journal, which helped declutter my mind and reveal unresolved issues. At first, I was resistant to the idea of forgiveness, but my gratitude journal prepared me for the process.

The benefits of forgiveness are huge, including emotional healing and feeling lighthearted. I was ready to learn to forgive so I could create a fresh start and feel free to pursue my passions with renewed and refreshed energy.

A fresh start is when we forgive completely and unconditionally, in our hearts and minds. Then we can transform our lives by using forgiveness; we can repair our health, work, and relationships, and attain a better quality of life.

We can let go of the past: emotional pain and damage, guilt, blame, grudges, depression, sadness, hurt, anger, resentment, and hatred. All these are temporary feelings that can be turned around. I used to be full of the past. I was dwelling on old emotions and traumas, and I was missing the joy of the present moment. I had a strong desire to become open to new input, thoughts, perceptions, and energy.

I was haunted by the thought that I had to let the painful past go, but I didn't need to dig into myself to look for those emotions and situations. They were right in front of me, as if saying, "Deal with us."

I found myself thinking about my beloved grandmother and remembering her wise words: "If someone hurts you, never hurt him or her back. Do something good for that person. Give people who hurt you a second chance." This saying guides me through my life, and I strongly believe it works. She taught me love, kindness, and compassion.

I also found myself thinking about how to understand myself better and get along with myself, and at the same time, recognizing that I still had anger and painful memories that stung when I thought about them. Sometimes I felt sad, mad, and frustrated. I didn't want to fight back or run away from pain, emotional wounds, and being hurt anymore. I also didn't want to close myself off from new experiences and people, and the good and beautiful that life offers. I just longed to be able to accept life the way it is, forgive myself and others, stop talking and thinking about what happened a long time ago, stop it from hurting me, let it go, and move on.

I used to think that it's a waste of time and energy to relive old traumas and unpleasant memories. I still think that's true. But to release the past, I must be willing to forgive everyone, including myself, completely. I must go through these traumas and memories one last time and then leave them in the past. I can change my attitudes, perceptions, and thoughts toward the past. Then I can move on and live my life joyfully.

Sometimes I think I'm being silly or unreasonable to punish myself now because someone hurt me in the past or my reaction was harmful to myself. Ruminating on a past conversation sparks a memory and takes me in a wrong direction. I have two choices: to stay in the past, suffer, and continue whining and making excuses, or put the past in order, enjoy the present, and move toward a blissful future.

Now, I can do my best to repair what was broken, using the tools I've discussed earlier, such as writing in a gratitude journal and forgiving. These are very powerful techniques, and they can be used for different purposes.

The time was right to create a ritual to say goodbye to inner pain, cleanse my mind of negative thoughts, and remove emotional clutter from my system. I could release my deepest thoughts and feelings about a particular situation. I could also explore my hidden desires and try to see things from different angles.

I continued this process with self-forgiveness, by forgiving myself for blaming others for mistreating me, thinking badly about someone, and saying hurtful words. Every time I thought of painful memories, I felt sorry for myself. Then I stopped myself and directed my thinking toward looking for what good I created from that experience and how the situation changed for the better. It might be that I learned something from it and would never behave the same way again. It might be that I was guided to develop new and valuable qualities. My past helped me understand more and become the person I am today. There were important life lessons to learn. I'm thankful for them, and I take with me only good memories.

I forgive myself first for my mistakes, weaknesses, and ignorance; then I forgive other people. All of us have flaws and imperfections, so we all feel guilty. We can always confess our weaknesses and forgive them.

After forgiving myself, I make a list of people I want to forgive for something they did or didn't do to me. I write on a piece of paper all the details and express my feelings about each person and situation. This makes me feel those emotions again. Then I read my list aloud and say, "I forgive this person for X. Now I understand that you didn't know better. I forgive myself for reacting the wrong way. At that time, I didn't know better either. We both did our best.

"I accept you the way you are. Maybe you were being protective of me. Maybe that experience was needed to transform us and push us in the right direction. Maybe it helped us learn something and changed our point of view.

Maybe you had a reason for your behavior that I didn't know about." There are so many maybes I can think of as I assess and understand a situation better. One simple understanding makes a big difference. Then I burn that piece of paper and let the past go.

When I replay a hurtful situation in my mind, it brings to the surface painful emotions that were caused by this situation. It's as if my mind is talking to me through pain because it's longing to achieve balance and harmony. Sometimes when I forgive totally and unconditionally, tears stream down my face, and I feel emotionally cleansed. I'm thankful for this moment of forgiveness. Emotional pain is melting more and more every time I practice forgiveness.

In the past, for whatever reason, I allowed emotional pain to enter my system. Now I've learned how to expel it and how to deal with it in the future (writing in my gratitude journal and talking to myself). This process heals and cleanses and leaves me fresh, new, and free. I visualize this person and their goodness, thank them for this experience, see them happy and content, and send them love and joy.

Forgiveness helps create calmness in the mind, unblocks roads to new achievements, and brings more happiness, joy, and positivity. Forgiving is liberating and makes me feel incredibly light. By using this simple tool, I've cultivated a forgiving heart filled with hope, love, kindness, and compassion. I've become kinder and more compassionate to myself and others.

Learning how to forgive is a turning point in my life. I have stopped being critical and judgmental toward myself and others, and started enjoying life more. I accept myself the way I am, with my perfections and imperfections, allowing room for change; and I accept other people the way they are. I have become happier and healthier, more agreeable, and more serene. I can focus on what I want to create in my life. It's been a healing process. Now I believe that everything in the past happened for a reason—for my good. There's a bright side to even the most unfair situations. I must be willing to look for it and to concentrate only on the positive.

Consider practicing forgiveness. Embrace a new you—rejuvenated and ready for a fresh start. Be your authentic and wonderful self.

How can your life improve if you practice gratefulness every day?

CHAPTER 3

General Remarks about Positivity

*In order to carry a positive action, we
must develop here a positive vision.*
—Dalai Lama

Be positive. Be true. Be kind.
—Roy Bennett

Emotional Luxury

Let's enliven our lives with positivity. We've dealt with the
negative most of our lives, but we still dream of a wonderful life where everything is easy—a life of emotional luxury.
Emotional luxury equals emotional trust. We can achieve it
by becoming familiar with the sense of positivity, organizing a field of positivity around us, setting our outlook to be
happy, and leaning on the sweeter side of life.

Why don't we lure ourselves into a realm of pure positivity and manage to stay there? We need some kind of
foundation to stand on confidently and comfortably, which
is trust and a positive attitude. Trusting the flow of life is

the best tool we can use to make better life choices. A positive attitude has a magical quality—it restores our vitality and helps us feel lighter, freer, and more beautiful.

When we think positively, it means we trust the universe, and all our future events line up in a nice and positive way. When our beliefs are good and strong, they take us straight to success; they show us the right direction. I choose to believe that all my wishes will come true. It's just a matter of time.

Whatever we think and believe comes true for us. Our beliefs affect our feelings and actions. Beliefs are thoughts that we've convinced ourselves are true. Our beliefs come from what people tell us at school, in our families, and in the media. They are telling you one way of thinking. What's your way of thinking? You can learn this by examining your beliefs.

Things can change for the better when we believe in our value and in the good in the world, and expect to succeed in most things. Then we'll have more positive experiences and feel much better. First, we believe in good; then we see and feel good.

We tend to see negativity around us. If we acknowledge positive aspects everywhere, even in unbearable circumstances, we can see the world from a new angle—the angle of positivity.

Every day, search for the positive in yourself and your life situations. Notice beauty in the most ordinary things around you—in people, at work, on the street, or everywhere you go. Cherish your life, its beauty, its abundance, and its generosity.

Positivity is about trusting what comes forth. Trusting the process of life means trusting our inner guidance, cultivating a deeper relationship with ourselves, and accepting the natural flow of events, people, and circumstances. By accepting them, we can develop the habit of trust. Events are events, people are people, and circumstances are circumstances. They surround us, and we cannot change them. But we can observe everything neutrally. That tool can be used skillfully so we can enjoy life fully.

When I realized that I don't have to fight anything and that trusting and accepting things as they are is a perfect and simple solution, I put my mind at rest. I direct my undivided attention to the positive, to total health, and to vitality. I invest my energy in positivity, and I enjoy the ease and comfort of being positive. It is the healthiest and happiest realization for me.

When we dwell on the negative, we exude negativity and create unfavorable situations. Why would we want to do that? When we dwell on the positive and feed our minds with beauty and goodness, we exude positivity and create favorable situations. It's as simple as that.

We can't simultaneously walk around in two completely different worlds, negative and positive. We have to choose one. Remember, we get what we choose. Let's compare negativity and positivity, and see which benefits us more.

Negativity equals imbalance, poor health, lack of energy, fear, excuses, things taken for granted, low self-esteem, arguments, and disharmony. When we're in disharmony, we become weak and susceptible to negative comments. Negative emotions like anger cause imbalance and ill health. When we're out of balance, our sleep, work, and emotions are off. When we argue, we exchange negative vibes. When we talk about what's negative in our situations or gossip or judge, we don't improve things. After watching negative news, it's hard to be positive. Negative thoughts destroy our lives and drastically drain our energy. They're poisonous. They hurt us and drive us crazy. We can stop this by simply switching our attention to the positive.

Positivity is the key. Positivity is strength. It provides us with the confidence that we can change for the better. It also gives us energy, wellness, gratitude, compassion, joy, comfort, curiosity, mindfulness, vitality, and love. It brings novelty and freshness.

Positivity equals balance and harmony. When we're in balance, we work, sleep, and feel well. When we're in harmony, nothing bothers us. Positive thoughts, words, and emotions heal us, enhance our vitality, and bring magical events to us. A positive, relaxed, and easygoing attitude helps us make good decisions and get what we want effortlessly.

A positive attitude is also a very attractive quality. When we're in a positive mood, we emanate harmony and good vibes. It creates a peaceful environment around us where everything goes well. We have what it takes. People are drawn to us; they want to listen to us and be in our wonderful and uplifting company.

It's important to work toward positivity and rise above negativity. In any negative situation, I can always choose whether to be positive or negative. For example, if someone says something hurtful to me, it can stay in my mind for a while. Someone's negative mood can spoil my whole day.

As I react to it and dwell on it, it feels like someone rules my life. It feels weird and draining.

I can see two ways to respond. First, I react because my emotions are triggered, and I start having a heated argument, trying to defend myself, which leads to a very uncomfortable place that drains my energy and steals my time. Second, I do not react, I remove my involvement from the incident, and I rescue my precious energy and emotions. If I pause, I can choose how I want to respond. I pick the second way because I prefer to make my life simple, easy, and enjoyable despite any negativity.

Another good technique I've learned is cultivating a neutral or a carefree attitude. When I observe neutrally, I can see solutions more quickly. As soon as I see a toxic scene, I walk away. If I can't leave, I can still handle it well because I stay in my lane of comfort. I ignore any negative comments. I don't let anyone talk me out of my goals, dreams, and enthusiasm. Whatever negative is happening, it goes past me without touching me.

When I believe in the good and positive, and hope for the best, my confidence and resilience improve. I can adapt to any situation more easily. I can change the direction of my thinking and be happy and content where I am. The best habit to develop is to meet everything that comes your way with positivity, gratitude, and acceptance. A wise quote by Swami Rama comes to mind: "Life doesn't need to be changed; only our attitudes do."

Developing this approach to life—living in contentment and doing everything with a good attitude—helps tremendously. I can move on with my day unattached to anything toxic and focusing only on my own path. The more I practice this, the more I like it, and the easier it gets.

I know that a positive attitude leads to positive life experiences. I cultivate more positivity with saying affirmations, having a book of desires, having inspirations, recalling happy times, doing motivational self-talk, and savoring.

Saying affirmations

What one imagines and affirms, one can create. Positive affirmations are statements describing how one wants one's life to be. Some affirmations are as follows: "Each day I get healthier with more energy," "My day is going well," "I'm doing fantastic," and "I'm in good spirits."

We can always start with one aspect of our life that we feel positive about. It's easy to dwell on it and draw positivity from it. We can say affirmations about that aspect, which improves our mood. Then that positive mood affects all other aspects.

Affirmations are always available. They can restore our health, shape our minds, help us realize our desires, and talk us into good intentions. They can help us overcome any obstacles, frustrations, or discouraging thoughts. They can also help us think positively about ourselves and others, and encourage us toward any goal. They're one way to shift our attitudes and perceptions. By using them, we can become familiar with a sense of positivity and be inspired to live healthfully.

Ten or twenty times a day, write down one or two favorite affirmations. Read them loudly, boldly, and enthusiastically. Repeat them about twenty times when you wake up in the morning and before you go to sleep. Go over them all day. When you're busy repeating them, it will help prevent negative thoughts from entering your mind. If they enter your mind anyway, just keep saying your affirmations. When you repeat affirmations and infuse them with feelings, they'll crowd out negative moods or comments. When affirmations are said many times, you have no choice but to accept them. It's surprising how powerful the repetition of positive statements can be. When we feed our positivity with supportive and encouraging affirmations and truly believe in them, they become our reality.

Having a book of desires

This book is a great, exciting, and powerful tool to help me clarify my wishes. I glue beautiful pictures in it according to every area of my life. I use these to attract everything from a chic wardrobe and nice furniture to good health, a warm relationship, and a successful career. I choose images that evoke feelings of love and make me happy. Some people use a vision board or a dream collage or a large piece of paper for display in a prominent space with pictures that represent desires and dreams and words taped on it. I prefer to keep mine to myself. I look at them often to keep motivation flowing.

Having inspirations

One of my favorite sources of inspiration and positivity is Esther Hicks, who channels as Abraham. I adore her philosophy; it focuses specifically on the positive things we can create. One of her messages is to see things as you want them to be. When I listen to her YouTube channel or read her books, it's always inspiring and cheering.

Recalling happy times

Whenever I start to feel a little low, I recall a time when I felt radiantly happy, such as during traveling or having a wonderful weekend, and I recall all the goodness in my life.

Doing motivational self-talk

I speak compassionately and respectfully with myself. Motivational self-talk, such as "You are doing famously" and "Keep going," can provide confidence and strength. When I replace inner discouraging talk with encouraging talk, I can meet any challenges better, I strengthen my resilience, and I do things that contribute to my health. This helps me let go of the negative and lightens my mood.

By doing this, I've noticed a huge improvement in my attitude. I've become calmer and more thankful for myself, others, and my surroundings.

Savoring

When we savor, we use our five senses and enjoy and appreciate our current situation. This increases gratitude and positive emotions. When we're grateful, we can recognize gifts, such as music and bird chirping, the beauty of the ocean, a delicious dinner or dessert, travel, a spa day, feel-good videos and movies, a baby's smile, and cute puppies and kittens. All these can instantly and naturally boost our mood. Create rituals around savoring. Make time for pleasurable activities. Practice looking for the good and savor wonderful people, music, books, and events.

Those are some tools I use to encourage positivity. Another tool is a thirty-day positivity quest, which can be an exciting and empowering adventure. For thirty days, prioritize your positivity. Adopt a new mindset, a positive and flexible mindset. Learn to think and speak in a positive manner. When positivity enters your heart and mind, it can improve your character and may even change your destiny. Think thoughts that make you happy, do things that make you feel good, be with people who energize and love you, eat food that makes you healthy, and go at a pace that allows you to enjoy the extraordinary beauty of life. Aspire to perform your daily tasks in the most pleasant way possible.

Live your life in beauty, ease, comfort, and positivity. Be willing to get acquainted with emotional luxury.

You probably think, *That's easier said than done. What am I supposed to do with all my scattered thoughts? How can I relieve the stress of life, get rid of emotional poison, be positive, and take time for rest and relaxation? How can I possibly do that?*

I've often had the same questions. We all have scattered thoughts and mind chatter. I had a strong desire to make peace with mine and achieve emotional luxury. I believed that if I could make peace with this chatter, I could gain confidence, perform better, accomplish more, and live healthfully.

Then one day, it happened. I encountered a great book filled with simple and practical meditations and techniques.

The first meditation I tried from the book was about how to unleash the inner chatterbox. Every night before I went to sleep, I was to sit facing a wall and talk to it for forty minutes. This felt strange. Then I had an idea. I could talk to an imaginary friend in the form of a wall. At first, I was shy and didn't know what to say. Then I recalled my day, the people I met, the interactions I had, the events, and the emotions; and I started to speak freely, describing what happened and how I felt. I discovered that I could talk for an hour or even two with feelings and gestures. I couldn't believe I could talk that long. Sometimes I even cried. That felt good; it was a sign of relief and emotional cleansing.

Every day, I liked this practice more. I began to rush home to talk to my friend. It was relaxing, comforting, and easy. I was astonished at how my mood improved. I also slept deeply and soundly. And I was able to get in touch with my deepest desires and aspirations. This technique motivated me, inspired me, and simply gave me joy. I could replace my inner chatter with pleasant and uplifting talk. I could do things that contributed to improving my health, work, and relationships. With this practice, I could move into a peaceful state of mind. It helped me become my own source of calm and encouragement.

Everyone desires peace of mind. But how many of us obtain it? I know that if I change my mental patterns and redirect my attention, I can see a different and better picture of my life. When the mind is free of clutter, we can receive new thoughts. When we get rid of emotional rubbish, we make room for emotional luxury.

If mind chatter is your concern, you may enjoy this technique, which is like a conversation with your inner self. It helped me, and it may help you too.

Read "Unleash the Inner Chatterbox" from *Pharmacy for the Soul* by Osho.

If a continuous inner dialogue is there, it must have a cause inside. Rather than repressing it, allow it.

Through allowing it, it will disappear. It wants to communicate something to you. Your mind wants to talk to you. Something you haven't been listening to, haven't been caring about, or have been indifferent to wants to relate to you. You may not be aware of what it wants to relate to you because you've always been fighting it, thinking it's crazy, and trying to stop it or convert it into something else. All diversions are a sort of repression.

Do one thing. Every night before you go to sleep, for forty minutes, sit facing the wall and start talking—loudly. Enjoy it and be with it. If you find that there are two voices, then talk from both sides. Give your support to this side, then answer from the other side and see how you can create a beautiful dialogue.

Don't try to manipulate it because you aren't saying it for anybody. If it's going to be crazy, let it be. Don't try to cut anything out or censor anything because then the whole point is lost.

Do it for at least ten days, and for those forty minutes, in no way try to be against it. Just put your whole energy into it. Within ten days, something will surface that has been trying to tell you something but you haven't been listening, or there will be something of which you were aware but didn't want to hear. Listen to it, and then it's finished.

Start this talking to the wall and be totally in it. Keep the lights either off or very dim. If sometimes you feel like shouting and becoming angry in your talk, shout and become angry, because it will go deep only when it's done with feeling. If you're just on a head trip and you go on repeating words like a dead tape, that won't help, and the real thing won't surface.

Talk with feeling and gestures, as if the other is present there. After about twenty-five minutes, you'll warm up. The last fifteen minutes will be tremendously beautiful. You'll enjoy it. After ten days, you'll see that by and by, the inner talk is disappearing, and you've come to understand a few things you've never understood about yourself.

A Brunch to Remember

Be the attitude you want to be around.
—Tim DeTellis

It was a sunny Sunday morning. I had a day off. I was anticipating an interesting and relaxing day. First, I had to do some chores. Then I could do whatever I liked. I did an exercise routine and had a nice shower. While I was choosing what to wear, the phone rang. It was a friend, and she seemed sad or upset, maybe even tearful. "Let's get together and have a little chat over coffee at our favorite place," I said. She agreed eagerly.

We met at a cozy café with a beautiful water view. The coffee was delicious. I was happy to see my friend, but she was pretty unhappy; she was in a state of confusion. I felt that she needed some moral support, and I wanted to bring her out of her sadness and back to balance. My intention was to have a calm, pleasant talk and to offer warm words of encouragement to create a joyful atmosphere of comfort and have quality time together.

She told me that she'd woken up with no energy or desire to meet a new day. She was emotionally drained and exhausted, and couldn't even function, overwhelmed with loneliness, despair, and fear. Her depression was obvious. As I learned later, she was unsatisfied in her job.

She said that it was very important to feel good about what we did. She believed there must be a better alternative but found herself stuck in an unfulfilling job that she felt she couldn't quit yet. She wanted to find a good job with some flexibility that enhanced her quality of life. Even though she'd made a big effort to make her life better, she didn't see any improvement. She'd tried many times to change her job and financial situation, but something always blocked her. She had run after achievements but hadn't gotten the results she wanted. She didn't want to say she hadn't achieved anything; some of her efforts were successful. She tried to be cheerful and told herself not to worry; her abundance was on its way. She also told herself to find a way to like her job, to accept that each job had its perks, and to embrace her current situation; but it was not really helping.

I can relate to that, and I'm sure many other people can too. We all face similar situations. I've thought about it a lot. Some things are fine and don't need to be changed. Some things can't be changed; they are what they are. I've pondered the wise suggestion that if you can change a bad situation, do so; but if you can't, accept things as they are and learn to trust them, even if you don't understand the reason behind that. I tell myself, *Just trust the flow of life.*

Also, accomplishments are good, but we need to be flexible about them. When we try desperately to achieve our goals because we want them so badly and want them to happen quickly, it creates great tension and actually blocks our route to worthwhile achievements. Give more energy to what we want to become and keep improving, learning, and growing. Sooner or later, our achievements will add up and satisfy our desire for accomplishments. Once we finish something, we usually look for another challenge anyway. I have concluded that it doesn't really matter whether I accomplish great things or not. The only thing that matters is what kind of person I become in the process—whether I enjoy myself and feel good about that situation, learn from it, and rectify mistakes. In any circumstance, we can always choose—to whine and be bitter and sad, or to be sweet and pleasant no matter what. The choice is ours. I choose to be the best person I can be.

There will always be negative voices in our heads that want to sabotage us. Ignore them and learn instead to pay close attention to the positive. Negativity is poison; don't let it into your mind. Positive energy rekindles; it feels good. We all have beautiful and happy thoughts and intentions. Don't hide them. Bring them to the surface.

Fortunately, we have the power to transform any challenging situation into something more beneficial and uplifting. Let's have a much better quality of life.

Our coffee time turned into a healthy and delicious brunch. I suggested moving on and finding a way to see the positive and starting to think, speak, and act according to it. She was delighted to hear that and willing to do it too. We were on the same page. It's much easier to change a negative mood into a positive one when a friend supports it. I loved our positive twist.

We agreed on five topics for a rational conversation: gratitude, health, happiness, abundance, and energy. What made us happy? What could we do to improve our skills and talents? What made a good life anyway? We could become more familiar with ourselves and pay attention to what we want.

We talked about our interests and hobbies, our choices and strategies, activities we'd like to do, skills we'd like to learn, and education we'd like to pursue. What kind of people did we want to be? Confident, magnetic, or charismatic? What did we dream about? How did we unwind?

All that put us in a positive spirit. We were laughing and enjoying each other's company. We felt relief.

We started to create a plan of action toward new accomplishments. We established rules toward creating our best lives and discussed how to integrate them into our everyday routines. We planned to be kind and gentle with ourselves without rushing an outcome. We talked about steps toward achieving our goals and how to enjoy each step.

Once we found something we liked, we would stick with it. It became our ally; sooner or later, we would see the fruits of our labor. Results don't occur overnight; quick fixes don't exist. But we can fix our situation just by gaining clarity from a fresher and healthier perspective. The moment we let go of a situation of discomfort that we're attached to in an unhealthy way and pay attention to something more positive, the situation somehow resolves itself. The best thing is to try to feel good and enjoy the process.

Later that day, I was surprised by how quickly my friend's mood improved. Despite how she felt, we were able to use our words and intentions to change the perception of a situation just by talking about how we wanted it to be and what actions we could take. I'll always remember our lovely brunch together. We were able to step away from the unpleasant and into the pleasant just by switching our attention to the right and comfortable direction. My friend and I went home happy and positive.

Between Friends

*The most important thing you will
ever wear is your attitude.*
—Jeff Moore

I dislike conflict, and I'm very aware of others' moods. But with my close friends, I can relax. I strengthen relationships by learning more about my friends and their personalities, knowing things like whether they prefer to spend time alone or be in a crowd, if they prefer to go to the gym or take a yoga class, if they're sensitive, or if I can say anything to them. I notice what my friends and acquaintances like and try to be attentive to it. Life can be easier, simpler, and lovelier when we understand each other better.

I have friends for every category: a yoga friend, a sporty friend, a book-loving friend, and friends for different activities; one of my dear friends loves shopping. She could've been a great designer; she has exquisite taste. I love spending time with her, and if we're going to a mall, all the better. She's the kind of person I feel comfortable just being with. After shopping, we have lunch; drink coffee; eat chocolate; talk about fashion, style, and beauty; and just take pleasure in spending time together.

Another friend likes going to yoga and other classes with me. We learn how to live a healthy lifestyle, have a good philosophy, and fill our minds with beautiful, inspirational, and positive stories. We always have warm and encouraging talks.

My friends and I share similar interests. We opt to see the bright side of life. I don't hesitate to make my friends feel good when they need it. Good friends provide mutual support, advice, pleasant times, affection, and energy for living.

Sometimes I like to spend time with my friends, but other days, I like quality time alone to be conscientious about my agenda. I take some time for stillness. It can be a few minutes of having quiet time, slowing down, and developing my awareness of the present moment. I analyze my strengths and weaknesses, sort out issues, and try to maintain my energy. I consider moments of weakness times I should pause and reflect. During these pauses, I can focus on the positive. I can speak words of positivity, beauty, and comfort, and direct them where I want my life to go.

The more good people I bring into my circle of life, the better. There are many wonderful people in the world. It's very important to remember that friends must be nonjudgmental and accept one another as they are, although we tend to be judgmental and gossipy. Judgment is toxic. Why would I judge if I know that it's toxic for me? Judgment has no place in my life. It's a huge waste of energy. I try not to judge people, gossip, or say a bad word about anyone because I know some people are forced by circumstances to act a certain way. I'd probably do the same thing in their place. When we're in balance, we don't care what other people say, wear, or do. I let myself think of people positively. I prefer to see the best in people. I respect their individuality. I really care about treating people with respect.

Having beautiful and supportive relationships with friends is absolutely fantastic. When you can count on friends who possess such qualities as honesty and compassion, and be surrounded with people who wish you well, it makes life comfortable, joyful, and balanced.

We're all different and have different opinions, but we agree on one thing: We truly want to live the best lives possible. When we believe in positivity, hope for the best, and trust the universe, we strengthen our resilience, cultivate more flexible thinking, and see more options. We can choose where to direct our attention. We're responsible for our perceptions about any life situation. When we see the world around us positively, we'll experience an abundant and positive world.

What's really important is how we feel. Positivity is emotional luxury. Positivity is magic. Play with this magic. By magic, I mean it's when we're able to feel good and to feel exhilaration for no apparent reason, wherever we go, whatever we do, and whoever we meet. When we smile, laugh, are in a lovely mood, and are grateful and compassionate, it means we're in balance. I won't barter my happiness for anything.

Trust, believe, fill your time with goodness, and stay healthy. Life is sweeter on the positive side. Emotional luxury feels awesome.

Do you agree that positive thoughts and habits attract positive results?

CHAPTER 4

General Remarks about Happiness

The purpose of our lives is to be happy.
—Dalai Lama

Happiness is not something you
postpone for the future, it is something
you design for the present.
—Jim Rohn

Lavish Happiness

Happiness isn't when I jump up and down and yell, "I can't believe this is happening to me!" That's just my reaction to a situation I don't feel ready for. It's definitely not when I say, "When I buy a winning lottery ticket, then I'll be happy," although I used to say that. I used to buy a ticket, hoping for a miracle. I think it's phenomenal to win the lottery. But first, I'd need to prepare for a financial windfall and a richer lifestyle. I'd also need to develop expensive taste. What's the point of winning millions if I still shop at ninety-nine-cent stores and don't know what to do with such an unexpected event? Meanwhile, let's get back to our favorite topic.

Happiness is more sophisticated than jumping and yelling; it's peaceful and poised. Happiness originates within ourselves. It's a sense of quiet joy and comfort, and a little smile of contentment. Happiness is being at peace with yourself and who you are.

Happiness is when you feel good despite what's going on around you and when you're calm even in a storm. It's a satisfying sense of peace that can sustain you through any life challenges and help you make the best of any situation. Happiness is when you're engaged in a hobby or work you love and you lose track of time.

Happiness is inner work. This work concerns our feelings about and perceptions of people and situations. It also involves introspection about the quality of our lives and our satisfaction with such parts of our lives as home, work, and relationships. For me, the essence of a happy lifestyle is when I can savor my daily tasks and do them with a sense of joy.

Happiness concerns the connection and the balance between our mind and body. If we desire a lifestyle that leads to health and happiness, we must be engaged with three main areas: positivity, nutrition, and exercise.

Happiness is interrelated with our sense of purpose. Everyone is seeking both happiness and purpose. When we live with purpose, it leads to happiness. Our purpose starts where our passion is—whatever brings us joy and bliss. We find our purpose when we freely accept our gifts and talents, make time for them, nurture and develop them, be patient with them, and let them blossom and grow organically. When we work in the field of our true passion, it feeds us with positivity and enthusiasm.

When we believe that we can create whatever we truly want, we're motivated to act and persevere.

Our levels of happiness can't always remain the same. They fluctuate, which is absolutely normal. I experience sadness and unhappiness from time to time, but it doesn't interfere with my overall happiness. I actually find some beauty in being sad. Those moments and even days of sadness are trying to say something to me or redirect my attention to a new and more important area or just move me to stop and smell the roses.

During a period of sadness, I just embrace everything that comes my way and take good care of myself, do what I like, listen to happy music, buy some beautiful flowers, and spend that time at a nice, slow pace. I enjoy being on my own and finding something to do that makes me happy or spending time with people who have a positive and supportive attitude, which helps me get into a better mood. When I think positively, I attract more positivity. The beauty of it is that it can be done instantly. Just by shifting my attention, I can be reconnected to the flow of happiness. I act as if I were already happy. It's all about mental attitude. How I think affects how I feel. I take sad moments and turn them into gratitude and favorite moments.

Can happiness improve our health? I strongly believe it can. From my experience, negative emotions, like fear and anxiety, can trigger health troubles. When I pay attention to something unpleasant, it can bring on a headache or another negative physical feeling. To avoid that, I deliberately think of something pleasant, which enhances positive emotions that can dramatically improve my mood and health. For example, I stop to notice good and beautiful things, and I use encouraging self-talk.

The more I enjoy and appreciate my lifestyle, the better it is for my overall health. The presence of abundant positivity and gratitude protects health.

Happiness is a way of life. Being in a happy and buoyant mood and profiting from the positive is our choice. When we feel uplifted, we're more likely to be attracted to a wide range of healthy activities and the more vital, meaningful, and happier our lives will become. When we're in a state of balance, we can judge our quality of life better. We move in the right direction—the direction of wellness. We start making wise and healthy choices in life, set the course of our lives for health and happiness, and don't settle for less.

I got most of my advice for how to be happy from self-help literature. I've read many books and magazines on the topic, gathering information to develop my own style of happiness. Some of them were redundant, and I didn't learn anything useful, while others were very interesting and full of true and practical information, which I incorporated into my life with pleasure. You might enjoy reading them. I have shared a list of them in "Suggested Readings."

When I find true and positive messages, I test them and come up with my own realizations and suggestions that fit me perfectly. I never know when a quote or phrase will touch my heart. Each source can help and has something to offer. Books and magazines entice us with promises and delights about the future, reinforce our hopes and beliefs, and help us perceive things more clearly and beneficially.

One of the messages in this literature was the idea of pursuing happiness. I didn't get it at first. I thought, *Why should I pursue happiness when it's within me all the time? It's here right now.* Eventually, I realized that I could interpret the idea to mean pursuing mindfulness and activities I value and the healthy lifestyle I enjoy. That made more sense to me. I could remind myself what makes me happy. I could experiment with feel-good strategies, act on them with conviction, and appreciate all moments of everyday joy. A style of happiness and lasting fulfilment evolves gradually. I'm not in a rush. I like it gradually.

My Story

Happiness is a quality of the soul...not a function of one's material circumstances.
—Aristotle

I can't help but wonder: Do the same kinds of things make most people happy? I believe so. But what makes me happy? I used to link happiness to future goals and events. I'll be happy when I take a vacation. Happiness was always in the future, but when the future came, it didn't live up to my expectations.

At one time, I thought things like appealing clothes, pleasant surroundings, elegant entertainment, good-looking partners, money, nice things, traveling, education, intelligence, great weather, a shiny new car, a luxury condo or beautiful house, and fancy technology could make me happy. Of course, I was happy to some degree because all that added a gorgeous surface to my life.

I used to know very little about true happiness. Over time, I realized that happiness was not only around me but also within me. I noticed that when my life had become boring, I tried to add some extravagant ornament on the surface. I thought if I acquired material items or started a new love affair, I'd regain my former happiness. These did have some effect, but as lovely as they were, they couldn't create long-lasting happiness. When the novelty wore off, I had to start all over again. As I learned, a better path to happiness is to find out what makes me really, truly happy.

I'd been contemplating the way I live and happiness for a while. Then one day, I was sitting in the waiting area of my favorite spa. There were wellness magazines on the table, and I took the Open Center catalog and browsed through it. My eyes stopped at a course called Certified Applied Positive Psychology (CAPP).

Positive psychology is the scientific study of human happiness. It teaches us how to be happy. This field of study is mainly concerned with how to achieve mental health and what makes people feel good, rather than what makes them feel bad. It's about building what's right for you, instead of fixing what's wrong with you.

I took the class because positive psychology was exactly what I craved. I longed to master the art of being happy. Although some of the material was too scientific for my taste, I loved every minute of the course. I simplified the information in order to use it in my life in the easiest and most enjoyable way possible.

The class included many wonderful subjects to explore and understand, such as the history of happiness, positivity, shifting mindsets, optimism, resilience, character strengths, flow, gratitude, sleep, physical activity, and nutrition.

According to the course, happiness is a subjective experience, but we can measure our happiness by seeing whether we're satisfied with our lives. Life satisfaction can only be judged by each person for himself or herself.

I take time to collect facts; then I can make major decisions. Once I decide, I commit to and nurture my personal growth. Real growth involves a period of confusion, pain, and even suffering before a new direction evolves because when we learn something new, it takes time to process and familiarize ourselves with it. This offers a really worthwhile challenge. It takes time, commitment, and dedication. It's a wonderful journey. The happiness quest itself is actually more exciting than reaching the goal. Although reaching goals feels awesome, it's always a work in progress. After taking the positive psychology course, I said to myself, "This was the beginning of my growth."

Happy people plan actions,
they don't plan results.
—Dennis Waitley

I had a true curiosity about life and perfect happiness, and positive psychology gave me the opportunity to learn how to be a happy person. When I said "gave me the opportunity," I meant that it showed me resources. I could see this opportunity as a path to happiness and prosperity. I had to really want to achieve happiness and be willing to put in the work to reach it. I was grateful for a chance to learn something new. I enjoyed the course and learned a lot. My final assignment was a presentation about what happiness means to me.

What does happiness mean to me? My beautiful mom always says, "Darling, you have only one obligation in life—to be happy." Being reminded of this many times helped me discover exactly what activities increase my happiness. It's a pretty long list: walking by the ocean, eating well, reading inspirational books, meditating, going to a concert, watching a favorite show, planning my next vacation, beautifying my home, simplifying my life, having a sumptuous lunch with a favorite person, having a good conversation with a friend, taking literature classes and educational workshops, getting spa treatments, and going on yoga retreats. I prefer activities that take longer because they're more gratifying and life-enhancing. The true measure of happiness is how I satisfy myself with my life. I pick one thing I can do every day to make me feel happy and healthy. I'm not rushing life because I'm really happy where I am.

I also practice giving, compassion, and gratitude. These lead to joy. A small wish of happiness or an appreciative thought for someone in my life has a huge impact on my own happiness as well. When I give happiness, I receive happiness. Giving always feels better than receiving. It also nourishes my mind-body balance. I enjoy cultivating happiness. Then I savor sharing it with myself and others. Generally speaking, I like doing something for myself and others daily. I also like to spend quality time with people who are like-minded and encouraging.

Studying positive psychology can help us find meaning in our lives, our relationships, and our work. I began to notice and develop my qualities, which led me to a deeper level of happiness. These qualities include humor, optimism, kindness, gratitude, generosity, curiosity, creativity, serenity, integrity, humility, originality, and courage. I enjoy addressing them one by one. Paying attention to the list below also enhances a positive mindset.

Happiness includes the following:

- Having a positive attitude toward myself and others
- Savoring little things, celebrating small wins, and praising myself
- Enjoying myself
- Fostering a sense of humor
- Being creative, curious, and grateful
- Giving generously of myself and my resources
- Viewing everything and everyone with gratitude
- Relishing a healthy lifestyle
- Having a simple, warm, and cozy environment
- Being on good terms with myself and others
- Writing in a diary

I was astounded to find myself such an interesting and engaging subject to study. I had the insight that small shifts in my daily thinking and perceptions, and wise and mindful lifestyle choices can put me on a positive path to contentment. I'm still evaluating what kind of lifestyle makes me truly happy.

With that in mind, I had the brilliant idea to make a thirty-day happiness pact with myself—a plan to discover happiness and get to know myself. I wanted to find comfort, confidence, true meaning, and peace within myself. I made a conscious effort to do it for thirty consecutive days and reflect on what I learned.

A happiness pact was reasonable. It helped me be more likely to appreciate positive aspects of life and do more things that I value and enjoy. Is a cup of coffee a source of happiness? Is yoga? Is watching the travel channel? We can always add more moments of happiness and replace an uncomfortable moment with a delightful one. Happiness depends on our approach to life. I like to keep in mind that life is very beautiful and magical, and look for more ways to feel that lavish sense of happiness.

I've gradually learned to anticipate a happy future, search my heart for values, keep what makes me happy in mind, and act accordingly. Everything I do in the present contributes to my lovely future, like planting positive seeds for a beautiful garden. In the long run, I'll develop a better attitude, which definitely leads to deeper and longer-lasting life satisfaction. Sometimes I feel a surge of happiness for no reason. These moments of happiness surprise me all the time, when nothing very exciting is going on. I'll be walking, and the sun will be shining brightly and the wind blowing pleasantly. When we notice and record these moments, happiness reveals itself.

Happiness is created by living a healthy, enjoyable lifestyle in which every day must be thought out well. I can always choose to be happy and remember that happiness resides within me. I just need to be more mindful, activate it, and focus on it.

Luckily, I can design my happiness in any form. I still like life's beautiful surface ornaments, and I also love self-exploration, introspection, and spirituality. I make sure to find a way to balance them and enjoy the extraordinary beauty of both.

We all search for happiness. Each of us has different ideas and expectations about it. Everything we truly desire is love, peace, health, joy, and purpose. Happiness is available to us right where we are. Anyone can lead a happier and healthier life.

Perhaps you'd like to explore your own happiness quest. It's worth finding out what makes you happy. A true perpetual happiness is waiting to be practiced and appreciated. When we feed off the energy of happiness, we project happiness into our reality and choose and enjoy being in that reality.

Living a life of happiness is actually the easy road to take. Once you've found your style of happiness, you'll live in happiness on earth.

A Spirit of Hedonism: Take Joy in Living

I finally figured out the only reason
to be alive is to enjoy it.
—Rita Mae Brown

One who likes fine jewelry and good clothes, eats sumptuously, thinks positively, and enjoys life can be called *hedonistic*. But is this really what *hedonism* means?

We can get into the spirit of hedonism. I'm not talking about the selfish pursuit of pleasure or immoderation. I'm talking about seeking pleasure in simple everyday things. We can always direct the spirit of hedonism into creating radiant health. We can seek pleasure in feeling healthy, positive, mindful, grateful, energetic, and beautiful.

What have you done for yourself lately? I'm sure you spend time and energy on friends and family. You're probably very good at making others happy. That's a good intention, but we can help others only when we have abundant vitality. Then we can share it generously and still have enough for ourselves.

There's no reason to feel guilty for putting yourself first. The most important intention is to love yourself enough to be willing to make time for yourself, which I call *self-love*.

You can take good and loving care of yourself and, of course, treat yourself with appreciation and respect. This is the first act of love, which leads to happiness. You can find a balance between your needs and other people's needs.

Turn your attention to what feels good. Prioritize hedonistic activities and really savor them.

Consider a new attitude for living your life. Imagine yourself at your best. Learn to love yourself. Have the desire to lead a happy life and take joy in everyday activities. It's worth developing a daily habit of feeling happy. You can create a healthy and joyful lifestyle in terms of eating well, drinking healthy beverages, exercising regularly, having goals, and staying positive no matter what.

It's simple and incredibly rewarding to live on love, pleasure, joy, vitality, gratitude, humor, and optimism. We can build a better life that charges us with passion, creativity, and originality. Allow yourself to be in the spirit of hedonism, radiate with happiness, and relish every moment of your fantastic life. Anticipate goodness because an inspirational and happy life awaits you.

What does happiness mean to you? What makes you happy?

CHAPTER 5

General Remarks about Simplicity

I have just three things to teach:
simplicity, patience, compassion. These
three are your greatest treasures.
—Lao Tzu

Clean Home, Clear Mind

My passion for creating assignments saved me at a difficult and stagnant time. I'm so good at creating assignments for myself; I'll never get bored. It was a time when nothing worked. The weight of life was overwhelming. I was emotionally drained by recent hectic events and financial insecurity. I was burned out with work and other demands. I was mentally tired. Something was telling me I should take it easy and simplify everything around me.

When I encountered any challenge, I perceived it as a lesson. This time taught me that it's helpful to channel my energy toward a strong distraction from my current issues and to concentrate on a new assignment. For the best results, I have to be diligent and vigilant. I also have to be capable of directing my attention to a different area and occupying myself completely with it, like cleaning and tidying my environment. I set myself, my home, my work, and my relationships on a path to wellness and moved through this time with grace and dignity. I find this process of simplifying life creative and satisfying.

I was beginning to wonder about simplicity. When I keep things simple, I have more time on my hands, and I can spend it as I like. I can always use more time. My plan was to get rid of junk and clutter, create a mess-free environment, and take pride in my home. My goal was to simplify my life, and have fewer things, and at the same time, free myself from any negative attachments. I could clear and refresh space both physically and mentally. I had a goal, and I was ready to find tools to achieve it.

My environment can be messy or neat, negative or positive, or simple or complicated. Investing in beautiful, harmonious surroundings can contribute to my healthy and happy lifestyle. It can help bring comfort and good fortune into my everyday work, career, and relationships.

Do I tend to complicate things? Yes, I do. Then simplify. When it comes to emotions, the more cluttered my life, the more feelings of worry, fear, resentment, dissatisfaction, and lack of self-love accumulate.

I believe everything in life is connected, including a clean home and a clear mind. Mental and physical housecleaning is needed so I can see the beliefs that have been running me. When I have a mess in my living space, it means I have a muddled head.

Clutter distracts when I try to concentrate and makes me feel like I'm stuck. Realizing this motivated me to choose a new beginning and to bring simplicity, renovation, and freshness to my home by cleaning and organizing and loving every minute of it. I discovered that renewing my environment was useful and even therapeutic, so getting rid of clutter benefits both my environment and my head. Life can be very complicated or simple and enjoyable. It's my choice.

What improvements can be made? How can I create a better quality of life? When I ask myself such questions, I'm filled with the energy to create solutions. I need to distinguish between what I need and don't need, and remove unnecessary items to create a more balanced surrounding, an elegant and simple style of living, and a more peaceful mind.

Each person has their own busy, beautiful, and cluttered space around them. Their home, work, material objects, friends, family, coworkers, pets, and the Internet—all that surrounds each one of us. It seems so overwhelming. If I thoroughly and lovingly clean and simplify everything I have, I'll feel better and freer. Then I can plan my schedule wisely. Speaking about schedules, I used to cram mine, and it made me tired and dissatisfied. I used to schedule events I didn't really want to go to. When I went to them, they weren't very interesting, and I regretted wasting my time. I learned from this mistake. It's not about doing less; it's about doing things wisely and thoughtfully, and enjoying them along the way.

I had to make many changes, let go of many things, clear my way to the new, simplify my actions in all areas, and prioritize only important things. My top priority is to focus on my inspiration, to be in harmony with myself, to try to be the person I want to be, to create a plan to achieve that, and to diligently follow it. When I don't have any inspiration, I spend some time alone to consider new directions and future moves. I take a weekend trip to a new place or enjoy one of my hobbies. Inspiration can come from anywhere. Inspiration encourages me and helps me persevere. I keep an inspiration list with fresh ideas. I just need to be flexible and open to new possibilities.

I truly believe that once I've simplified my life, everything around me will work toward my success. We get what we believe. I can start using my time and energy wisely and successfully, and devote myself to the things that really need my attention.

Technology is a big part of our lives. It deserves our attention. As part of my decluttering process, I want to take a look at technology and see how I can simplify its effect on my life.

Fancy Technology

You affect the world by what you browse.
—Tim Berners-Lee

Today, we have an incredible amount of alluring technology. Much is going on in this area. Technology feeds us a glut of information that's impossible to digest. Fancy technology is brilliant and very selfish at the same time. It's a huge burden mentally and physically. It consumes our time and drains our energy quickly without us noticing. I'm not anti-technology—far from it. I'm for using it wisely and beneficially. The energy of technology can be destructive when it's used in excess, or it can be very rewarding when it's used in balance. As for me, I try to be vigilant and not let virtual reality override actual reality.

Learning about different issues can be very interesting and also tiring. Can I distinguish good information from misinformation? Probably not. What I can do is to ignore any negative and unimportant information and take notice of only good and valuable news. I can stay in my lane of goodness and focus on my priorities, such as positivity, and learn useful and encouraging topics, which lead me to a better place.

Spending hours in front of a computer isn't my style, although I like Instagram because it supports my love of taking beautiful photos. I share my love for wellness on my website and blog, and I try to convey my passion for healthy and happy living. I give simple, practical tips about nutrition, exercise, gratitude, relaxation, and positivity—an inspiring and healthy lifestyle. I want to relate my experience and knowledge with people and help them shift their attention to excellent overall health. It's a wonderful way to send positive vibes to other people and the world. I enjoy doing this.

Few times I've been hypnotized by fancy technology. Too much of it makes me forget to eat, drink, and even clothe myself properly. The virtual world can be a mesmerizing place, as well as dangerous or terrifying. I rarely read the news because it tries to sell negative ideas. I'm not interested in it. However, people are eager to tell me about the news. Some people find other people's tragedies entertaining. I'm not interested in that either, although I have compassion for people.

The media are very important to us. They are a great source of information, but they also have some disadvantages. They can have a powerful effect on their audience. They take a negative or frightening story and dwell on it in great detail. A single message can even cause some people to panic. A negative message triggers negative emotions. A big part of information is destructive. I've realized it takes my attention and energy in a completely wrong direction because it's all about scary stories and aggression. I don't want to be a puppet and let the negativity be a puppeteer. I stay away from toxic influences. When I ignore them, they're powerless over me, and I can keep my emotions in balance. I believe that what I read and think is what I am. I prefer to live my story, be open-minded, rejoice in day-to-day reality, and cherish positive information. That's my style of steering away from bad influences. There's more to life than participating in chaos.

I'm very grateful for the benefits of technology. I can learn about good things happening in my city and the world, movies to watch, museums to visit, events to attend, places to go, and education to obtain. But I'm very selective in what I watch, read, and listen to. I love watching the History, Discovery, and health channels. I also love watching YouTube. I can find a wealth of useful information there. It inspires, educates, and entertains me. I try to focus on the positive more because I truly believe in the power of positive thinking.

On the other hand, I have a lot of free time when I'm not browsing the Internet. I take technology-free weekends, and once or twice a week, I leave my phone in another room or at home when I interact with nature or friends.

I find ways to balance, simplify, and of course, enjoy my relationship with enticing technology.

Fancy technology forces me into an unnatural way of living, and I try to remember the exceptional beauty of nature, as well as warm conversations in person rather than online. Although, it is absolutely miraculous that we can communicate through the Internet. It's fast, convenient, and breathtaking. As for me, I prefer less of the sophistication of technology and more of nature's beauty and abundance.

My Story

Life is really simple, but we insist
on making it complicated.
—Confucius

There are moments in life when I have to pause and reflect. I remember perfectly a day when I was journaling. All of a sudden, I stopped and looked around. The room seemed different, not as comfortable as it looked before. I had a sense that my environment was complicated and a little messy. Something triggered me to get up and go through my cabinets and closets and to open the door widely and see what I had and what I should get rid of. Something seemed to be saying, "You can do better." I was standing in the middle of my living room thinking, *What is this about?*

It's amazing how quickly I accumulate things. I've spent a lot of money on things that don't matter to me. Also, clutter creates stagnation, so that energy can't flow.

Twice a year, I declutter. I love doing this. I use a simple approach: If I like it, I keep it. If I dislike it, I toss it.

Even though I'm happy with my surroundings, that makes them even better. I can find things more quickly, I can get my space back, and I can be pleased with my environment. I can keep elegant and practical things, freeing myself from the burden of unnecessary clutter.

Each belonging, such as clothes and junk mail, needs attention; and the more belongings I have, the more attention they require. They are time and energy stealers.

I realized the importance of home as the foundation of life. My home needed to be restored to the comfortable living place I adore. I examined my surroundings and decided to organize every corner of my home. Starting each day with a specific task, like cleaning out my bathroom cabinet, it keeps me busy, meditative, and creative. I started small, one drawer at a time, or one hour per day. I started on each room, from left to right then top to bottom. I made sure good energy could travel freely without being blocked.

I've turned to two extraordinary philosophies for professional assistance: feng shui and Marie Kondo. These approaches help restore balance among possessions, houses, and people. They can be tailored to each individual.

Feng shui is a reliable source that's stood the test of time. It's the ancient Chinese system of creating harmonious surroundings, which brings serenity, prosperity, and good health. It's the art of arranging our belongings to facilitate the flow of positive and auspicious energy in our lives. The purpose behind feng shui is to balance the chi (vital energy) where we live and work and of people and places we see often. This precious energy, which circulates around all things, must flow freely.

I made a simple inspection of my furniture to see if it was too close together or if it got in my way. I followed this same approach throughout my home. I could even work on a specific aspect of my life to improve it (work, romance, money). My main goal was to make everything clean and neat. I wanted to transform my home into the home of my dreams.

Marie Kondo believes in the life-changing art of organizing and tidying up. I do too. She says that "When you put your house in order, you put your affairs and past in order too." I've enjoyed reading her book *Spark Joy*. It's full of simple and practical tips, which I gladly incorporated into my style of cleaning and simplifying.

In a sense, I am my home. I've developed a certain style over the years. I prefer expensive minimalism over cheap clutter. It's worth buying better things. In the long run, quality overrides quantity. My preference was the inspiration for this project. The project was to keep my home clean and in simple, cozy order.

I took an objective look at my space to see where I could clear away clutter, stagnation, and dust, and allow chi to flow freely. The best sequence for me was to start in the kitchen and dining room, then bathroom, bedroom, living room, closets, papers, and souvenirs. Speaking of the kitchen, decluttering that room helped me organize food, be more attentive to what I eat, and make easy access to things I use more frequently, while putting items I used infrequently in the back and getting rid of things I didn't use at all.

Every part of my life deserves quality attention. My closets were no different. They had been waiting for my undivided attention. I used to own a lot of clothes. When I opened a closet, it was hard to pick an outfit to wear. Even with a full closet, I would still say, "I have nothing to wear." Sometimes, it was hard to let things go because I was attached to them, but I started to do it anyway. I wore an outfit once or twice. If I loved it, it stayed. Otherwise, it had to go. During that process, I even learned how to put outfits together for a better look. It feels great to open a closet and know exactly what I want to wear. After all, looking good and feeling great are expressions of a lovely mood.

I only kept clothes that cheered me up and looked beautiful on me. I arranged my closet neatly on hangers by color, creating sections for dresses, jackets, skirts and pants, bags and belts, and shoes.

Things that had sentimental value, such as photos and photo albums, I kept but reduced in number. By the end of each week, I had one or two bags to donate to charity. It took me a few months to simplify. I felt pleased that I'd accomplished so much.

I enjoyed making positive changes in simple, effective, and creative ways. The changes were profound; they gave me peace of mind and helped me live in a more inspiring environment. As a bonus, my home was immaculately elegant. I felt that I was in a different, much better, and more relaxed place.

Simplicity is the ultimate sophistication.
—Leonardo Da Vinci

By being involved in this process of simplifying all areas of my life, I've come to understand that we all go through different life situations and, at the same time, similar situations. Sometimes we don't know how to deal with them and where to even start. I say consider the ultimate sophistication, which is simplicity. Da Vinci cannot be mistaken.

As I decluttered my lovely home, I felt a better energy flow. I began to feel healthier and more comfortable. Now my surroundings are adorable, my closets are awesome, my space is clean and cozy, and I have beautiful, fresh flowers in a vase. A few simple changes can make a real difference. My home greets me in a positive way every time I open the door. At the end of the day, it brings me a lot of pleasure, joy, and calmness. Home sweet home.

I take pride in my enlivened home. As I write this, I'm sitting by the window in a very comfortable chair, drinking delicious hot tea in a clean, quiet, and absolutely beautiful room. At moments like these, I can hear my heart beat, and I listen to what it has to say. It's probably preparing me for my next assignment.

It was essential to create a peaceful space in which I could evaluate my next step in life with a clear mind and get ready for it. My next step was to get acquainted with the energy of money and establish a friendlier relationship with it.

Do you agree with the statement "clean house = happy life"?

CHAPTER 6

General Remarks about Money

Wealth is not his that has it
but his that enjoys it.
—Benjamin Franklin

Formal education will make you a living; self-
education will make you a fortune.
—Jim Rohn

The Energy of Money

How many of us know how to treat the energy of money? Unfortunately, they don't teach that in schools.

Gold, silver, and copper have been the most popular kinds of money throughout the centuries. In today's world, money is made of paper, which has almost no value in itself. But we give that paper value; the popularity of paper money is undeniable.

I went through a seven-year financial drought. Everything I did to improve my financial situation failed. Every door and every window of opportunity was closed, as if some kind of power much bigger than me had done so. Every move I made was doomed. My first reaction was that I was a victim. "It isn't fair." I remember sitting on my couch looking at a pile of bills. I had a debt that was weighing heavily on me. I was devastated. I didn't know whether to laugh or cry. I'm sure this scene is familiar to many people.

Temporary financial problems can happen to anyone, but when we look on the bright side, no situation is entirely hopeless. If I put myself in this situation, I can take myself out of it. I embraced a challenge, and persisted in the face of adversity. My plan was to become knowledgeable about money, pay my debts, simplify my finances, and achieve the art of being on good terms with the energy of money. I want to share my observations on that fascinating subject.

Money is a terrible master but
an excellent servant.
—P. T. Barnum

We live in the material world. Money is something we have to deal with every day. Most things cost money. Money is usually defined as a medium of exchange. We receive it for the work we do and spend it on things we want and need. Money exists to serve us, not the other way around. It's for bringing joy and taking care of ourselves, by paying for our home, food, clothes, and more.

It's wonderful to feel free with money. It's not my style to deprive myself of pleasures like joining a gym or treating myself well. When I spend money, I always say, "Thank you for being so generous." It paid for educational courses, a great time with my friend at lunch, or travels.

I want to participate in the circulation of money. Money is meant to circulate. Its energy loves to circulate. It doesn't like to be imprisoned; it wants to go for a walk. When money doesn't circulate, stagnation forms. It's important to be giving and generous; this corrects stagnant energy around us. When we let this energy of money go freely, it always comes back to us. If we aren't respectful of it, it will leave us. It has a mysterious way of disappearing and reappearing. When we give to others, we're also giving to ourselves. When we share the flow of money intelligently with ourselves and others, it always finds a way to return to us.

My Story

It is how you deal with failure that
determines how you achieve success.
—David Feherty

Clearly, I was in a weak period. It was time to observe and learn instead of worry, fear, and resent. In times of difficulty, some kind of soul-searching comes naturally. After getting tired of looking at my bills, I started to teach myself simplicity and patience. No matter what issues I face, I always try to find the positive in them.

I became willing to examine what I was doing wrong so I could correct it. It seemed like money kept slipping through my fingers. It felt as if something had banned me from the path of prosperity, or maybe I didn't know how to allow the flow of the energy of money. Maybe I had a bad habit that contributed to my lack; if so, I wanted to replace it with a good habit that would contribute to my luck and affluence. Maybe it had to do with my mindset. Perhaps I could change that and start living easily. It was hard to throw away all my attachments to my current mindset, but I was willing to do a certain amount of inner work. Or maybe I kept money from coming to me with wrong thoughts. It was definitely time to change permanently from thoughts of lacking to having a vision of abundance. I made the decision to explore my thoughts and feelings about money, think more consciously and positively about it, get as much information as I could about it, choose financial freedom, and get on a path to financial wellness.

While on that path, I had to learn how much money I really need. Money isn't only a physical form; it's also energy. Nowadays, we say that everything is energy. The sun is energy. The ocean is energy. As noted in Chinese philosophy, money is energy too. Any kind of energy can create or destroy. We can enjoy the energy of the sun, get a gorgeous suntan, and get all the benefits of that beautiful energy. Or the same energy can burn our skin to a damaging degree. The energy of money can put us in a stagnant and miserable place or it can reward us with its abundance and wealth. It depends on how we treat it.

The best suggestion is to read a manual and see what to do and what not to do. That manual hadn't been written yet, so I had to write my own. I did a lot of research about money. I was determined to learn how this energy of money wants to be treated. What does money like? How do I establish a great relationship with its energy? How do I get to know it better and show my love and respect so it can love me back? How do I interact with the energy of money differently and lovingly? How do I get money to come to me easily and often?

*It is not the man who has too little, but
the man who craves more that is poor.*
—Seneca

Money can be a sweet word. We can afford many wonderful things. But sometimes we're seduced by the energy of money to an unhealthy degree. We have two different kinds of love for money—negative and positive. A negative love for money is when one is obsessed with it. One envies other people's luck, hates people who have money, is afraid of letting it go, and feels stingy about it. By having these thoughts, one doesn't let wealth into one's life and blocks the flow of that peculiar energy of money. When one fears losing money, one focuses on its absence and becomes worried that it won't be there or that there will be less of it. Thoughts of the absence of money can bring a lot of suffering.

On the other hand, too much money can also bring suffering. The more one acquires, the more one desires. The desire for more possessions leads to greed and selfishness. It has a snowball effect. A golden medium or balance must be found. When one lets money have power over one's life, making and saving become the dominant factors for one's happiness. A strong desire to possess it creates a dependence on it. All one thinks of is how to get and save more. A strong desire to save money takes our attention away from enjoying life. We deprive ourselves of happiness, and the goals become saving and guarding. We think we're guarding, but we're simply worrying.

When we worry about things that are beyond our control, we waste our time. We think we're guarding our money, but that's an illusion. If you think a big sum of money in your bank is reliable security, think again. Banks can fail. Prices can go up. The purchasing price of money can fall.

There's nothing wrong with saving money, but a strong attachment to it can totally control one. Then saving actually overrides the joy that can come from things money can buy, like a concert or a box of chocolates. Saving money can become like a drug. One can be very addicted to it and completely obsessed with it. Being obsessed with and addicted to anything leads to the fear of losing it, which eventually happens.

For example, I bought a beautiful and expensive pair of boots. I adored them. I was obsessed with them. I was afraid of ruining them. I had a pedicure appointment one day. I took my precious boots off and put them in a place I thought was safe. I was admiring them and checking on them all the time to make sure they were all right. A woman was standing next to me, and we were talking. She was holding a cup of coffee. Another woman passed behind her and accidentally bumped her, and she spilled her whole cup of coffee right on my boots. I wasn't angry in that moment. I realized I was thinking negatively and emanating the wrong signal with my thoughts, the signal of worry and obsession. I focused on what I didn't want. It was very important to me not to damage my boots. I was thinking negatively about them. This was a good insight for me. When I worry, it creates a problem. When I'm relaxed, it creates ease. Things become less important to me. I had to return from being obsessed to being balanced. I learn from my mistakes quickly, and I try not to make the same mistake twice. Too much attachment and clinging equals losing. Having a carefree attitude toward anything but still being loving and caring equals keeping.

Interestingly, most of us believe and say, too, "I'll never have enough money. I'll feel better and more secure about money when I see it in my life and I have a lot of it." I used to have the same belief. I'd been creating a tight feeling by complaining about my lack. My complaints prevented a financial flow from happening; if I removed my negativity toward that topic, I could start living with an easy feeling. When I felt restricted about money, it sent that energy out, and it came back to me with more feelings of restriction. If I stopped giving my attention to such thoughts and stopped reacting to and supporting a situation of lack, my money situation would eventually balance out.

When we emanate negative emotions due to worrying about money, we attract the negative state of having less of it. A negative love for money, worries, and doubts usually leads to poverty. If we pay attention to negative thoughts about our finances and fear of losing money, they will be nourished and multiplied. If we don't pay attention, they will vanish quickly.

I used to make that mistake, talking poorly about money and entertaining a worst-case scenario, until I discovered a wise and practical statement. It was the Law of Attraction that changed my view on prosperity. Its message was simple: Stop focusing on lack and start focusing on abundance. I studied this law until I got it. It took me awhile. To attract better financial feelings, I must focus on wealth—then I'd attract wealth. It was as simple as that. I had to tell a different story—a positive one—about my situation.

This approach taught me to feel financially well whether I had money or not. I knew it would come when I needed it. I had found this insight fascinating. I had to feel and think better about money first, and then my finances would improve. Inner work must come first. I needed to change my beliefs about money. During this period, I calmed myself with yoga, a pleasant walk, or a nap. Whenever I started to worry, I did something I enjoyed instead.

Luckily for me, another source of help showed up; it was a book called *You Can Heal Your Life* by Louise Hay. Reading it was the beginning of my love of and appreciation for bills. I remember this book saying to love your bills and stop worrying about them and money. I kept saying, "I love my bills." At first, I felt awkward saying these words, but gradually, I felt more comfortable. It was my mantra until I totally believed in this message. I knew for a fact that a good and positive statement improved my mindset. This book also gave me a new and valuable perspective, for which I'm very grateful.

These philosophies of the Law of Attraction and Louise Hay have shaped my new attitude toward money. Once we envision what we want, we can achieve a level of financial comfort that frees us from everyday stresses over money, and we can enjoy the kind of lifestyle that makes us and our family happy (whatever that may be).

The positive love for money, which includes calmness and trust, leads to wealth. Being calm in a time of lack means trusting the process of life.

Positive thoughts toward money work like money magnets and can resolve any financial dilemma for good. When we emanate the right signal to the universe, it always returns the favor. I'm grateful for what I already have. When I emanate that gratitude, it's the right signal to send to the universe. The positive love for money concerns achieving the art of attracting, saving, spending, and enjoying it in a balanced and beautiful way.

The good news is that we have plenty of opportunities to change any situation for the better. Having a positive love for money is actually achievable when we begin to understand where our power lies and connect with that power. Our power lies in being willing to cultivate that positive love. Cultivation requires work.

Here are some practical suggestions for a better flow of money and a more positive attitude toward it.

- Be grateful for what you already have.
- Be attentive to money.
- Count it respectfully.
- Call it good names.
- Think of it positively.
- Put it neatly in your wallet.
- Learn to use it wisely.
- Support other people's goals.
- Share your ideas with only supportive people.

- Earn money with joy.
- Accept money for your work with gratitude.
- Ideally, get paid for a job you love.
- Look for and develop your talents constantly.
- Learn money management.
- Love money unconditionally but be detached from it.
- Allow it to come to you freely.
- Spend it with ease and joy.
- Be reasonable about saving and spending.
- Think about your goals, and money will come.
- Move toward success and prosperity.
- Study people who have reached financial freedom.
- Keep your home clean and spacious.
- Explore the hidden secrets of the universe through world philosophies and the Law of Attraction.
- Be giving. What you give, you give to yourself. Also, what you say to others, you say to yourself. What you wish for others, you wish for yourself.

I can see a strong link between a healthy lifestyle and personal prosperity. When I take good care of myself, I have fewer money worries. My mind is occupied with being mindful, eating well, exercising regularly, and being grateful for what I have. And when I'm mentally and physically well, it affects how much I earn and how well I manage money.

There's also a strong link between a clean and uncluttered home and the flow of money. In a clean environment, the energy flows favorably.

Life is full of wonderful gifts and surprises that we can enjoy. When money comes, I love spoiling myself. It's good for my mood to go to a ballet, listen to beautiful music, see art, or be generous to someone. Money brings joy, a feeling of fun, ease, interest, love, and balance. I'm not talking about squandering money. I don't do that, and I don't skimp either. Ether squandering or saving every penny creates imbalance. I'm looking for a sensible way to find balance.

> *Money is only a tool. It will take*
> *you wherever you wish, but it will*
> *not replace you as the driver.*
> —Ayn Rand

Most importantly, I learned that money isn't a goal. It's a tool for accomplishing my goals. I prefer to think more about my goals than about money. I don't need to pump up my savings or slim down my spending. Abundance can be in the form of health, love, work, and peace of mind. It's good when I'm motivated by my goals. I have a vision of what I want to accomplish. I make a plan, and then money comes to support it. Some people are motivated to accumulate as much money as possible. I've tried that, and it is the wrong direction for me.

When I started to feel better about money, I attracted better and more comfortable financial feelings, and the truth about money's energy started to reveal itself to me bit by bit. I stopped feeling tight and restricted about money, and I learned how to focus on prosperity. I began trusting that everything was working perfectly, and I felt peaceful with my daily life. My money stagnation has been alleviated, the energy of money has been flowing better, and my life has changed in a positive direction. Financial ups and downs no longer threaten me. I know how to handle them.

Now I can answer the question I asked earlier in this chapter: How much money do I really need? Different amounts of money work for different people. As for me, the amount of money is unimportant, as long as it covers expenses and leaves something extra. The most important thing is to trust and feel calm about it and to find the right way to spread it evenly; first, to pay all your bills on time, then see what you have left, and distribute it wisely. Once you learn how to manage what you have, you will get more.

When I have money, I rejoice. I'm fine. When I lack money, I do the same. I'm fine then too. I consider myself a happy person because I'm content with what I already have, although, of course, I'm eager for more.

Looking back on my financial drought, the years of hardships taught me a lot and shaped my character. I feel grateful for that, as well as for learning how to treat money: with love, respect, and positivity. I've tried to be a good student who wanted to learn and understand how the energy of money and abundance works and how to make the right decisions about spending and saving. It was a beautiful process of self-introspection and self-education. I've endured my financial obstacles by analyzing my views about money and educating myself on the exceptional energy of money. I've entered a better period of my life. My financial lack turned into financial luck. It was a perfect way to start transforming my life toward more wealth.

The joy of financial freedom awaits us when we're willing to move that joy forward. When I want to change, my life changes accordingly. One of my favorite affirmations is "I have the financial freedom to be, to do, and to go as my heart desires."

An investment in knowledge
pays the best interest.
—Benjamin Franklin

As for now, I pay my bills with pleasure. I feel grateful for the services they represent. They enable me to live the life I do. I dare say I've found my exclusive style of treating money energy well and have a better connection with that favorable energy.

Live life generously. Become a magnet for prosperity. Develop a great relationship with the energy of money. Stay in gratitude, abundance, and wealth. Trust life, with love and acceptance.

Do you agree that money is a friend who requires respect and proper treatment?

CHAPTER 7

General Remarks about Love

To live is to love, to love is to
give, to give is to have.
—Yogi Bhajan

Love Blossoms

I hear people say life's too short. Life is beautiful, and there's plenty of time to taste its flavor and enjoy it.

Life is a boomerang. Nothing escapes the keen eye of the boomerang effect. It's always at work. How you live your life—your thoughts and actions—is what you get.

Life is a wonderful journey. It's an unscripted adventure. Love and kindness are qualities of that journey. Instead of complaining about life, jump-start positive changes. There will always be possibilities, challenges, and solutions to find balance. What you think is what you create. When you stop taking life for granted, you can rediscover your inner capacity to cherish your life.

We can choose to create a life from a place of love. When we discover love within, we become familiar with everything that involves love. As a bonus, we can learn a lot about ourselves in that process because love is a journey of self-discovery.

Contemplate your life. Take a fresh look at how it's going. What's it about? What's really going on? Love life and yourself. Loving yourself is all about treating yourself with love, self-acceptance, and respect. Change the usual. Make room for the new and good in your life. Only you can elevate your life and make it extraordinary.

I've enjoyed traveling on my love quest. What have I learned about love so far? Love is sharing and caring. Love involves gratitude, creativity, wisdom, curiosity, joy, humility, positivity, loving yourself, authenticity, and kindness. All these can be cultivated and practiced. Also, love is beauty that makes your eyes shine and projects light from within.

The energy of love can transform us. It can help us see the world as brighter and kinder. Food tastes more delicious, our jobs become easier and bring small joys, music becomes pleasant and uplifting, and relationships become warmer. All problems seem solvable. When we're engaged in practicing love, love begins to blossom. We can enjoy our lives and recognize and appreciate our beauty.

People should be beautiful in every way—
in their faces, in the way they dress, in their
thoughts, and in their innermost selves.
—Anton Chekhov

We were born with inner and outer beauty. They exist in everyone and are expressed in the talents, creative work, strengths, manners, appearance, potential, and beliefs that make each of us unique. When inner and outer beauty align, it's natural to have a beautiful personality, by which, I mean kindness and gratitude toward ourselves and others.

We can spend a lot of time and effort grooming ourselves to improve our appearance. We can also spend a lot of time and effort discovering our inner beauty, which shines from within. Transformation happens on both the outside and the inside. Why not pour more time and energy into learning more about love and yourself? Why not discover a new you and keep it around?

When I realized that most people experience a lack of self-love, I no longer felt alone. Self-approval and self-acceptance are key to positive changes. If I don't love and accept myself as I am, I'm not motivated to change for the better.

Love has many faces; one of them is self-love. Self-love is often confused with selfishness, but it's not. We're selfish when we lack self-love. We try to take love from others to fill our emptiness. We think love is something others do for us and something we can't do for ourselves. When we know how to love ourselves, we don't feel empty. We feel fulfilled from within. We don't need attention from others. We're busy with a journey of self-discovery that is improving the quality of our lives.

Loving ourselves is our responsibility. When we do this, it shows that we know what we truly deserve and are willing to give it to ourselves. Self-love and acceptance influence us in a positive way. We can embrace our flaws and imperfections, as well as those of others, while working to improve ourselves.

My Story

You, yourself, as much as anybody
in the entire universe, deserve
your love and affection.

—Buddha

Do you want to meet the love of
your life? Look in the mirror.

—Byron Katie

We tend to focus on our flaws; we spend every day judging ourselves and others. We're very skilled at finding small blemishes and making them bigger. There's much more criticism and judgment than love.

The first step in making desirable changes is accepting myself. If I dislike myself, I must turn that around and develop true self-love and appreciation. I must treat myself well.

Gradually, I can achieve a positive self-image and be grateful for the way I am.

I've embarked on a journey of self-love and acceptance and kindness to myself. This journey includes feeling good about myself, embracing my appearance, nourishing my mind and body, dropping my negative self-image, and not criticizing myself and comparing myself to others. Instead, I want to see myself as strong, confident, and healthy. I'm willing to address that challenge and accomplish that interesting task.

I assess myself on a scale from 1 to 10. If I give myself less than 10, I don't love myself enough. It means I could use some help learning to appreciate and accept myself. To do that, I use a mirror exercise from one of my favorite books, *You Can Heal Yourself* by Louise Hay. She's helped many people improve their health and happiness, and create the life of their dreams.

One of Hay's techniques, which I call the positive mirror exercise, helps me recognize my value. I use either a large or small mirror. Every time I pass a large mirror, I say something positive about myself, like "It's good to be me," and blow myself a kiss.

When I use a small mirror, I take time to focus on discovering the real me, and I ask the question, "Are you happy?" I look into my eyes with kindness, study my face, and note any critical thoughts about my appearance. Then I say good things about myself, like "I love myself, and I approve of myself, my body, my life, and this wonderful day." Then I say it again, and this time, I try to believe it. Looking into my eyes and accepting myself is powerful.

> *To be beautiful means to be yourself.*
> *You don't need to be accepted by*
> *others. You need to accept yourself.*
> —Thich Nhat Hanh

My intention in doing this exercise is to focus on accepting and appreciating myself. I replace my self-critical thoughts with healthier and kinder ones. At first, it feels awkward complimenting myself, but when I get used to it, it starts to feel more natural and believable. Self-love and acceptance need to be expressed. I feel release and comfort when I say these things.

The goal of this technique is to work the muscle of positive thinking with compassion toward myself. Feeling positive about myself helps me be more compassionate toward others too.

Doing this exercise helps me say (and mean), "It's good to be me," and removes the need to compare myself to others. Prevailing images of what's stylish and popular create our perceptions of beauty. Health and glamour magazines sell the dream of quick fixes. When we see a gorgeous woman on a magazine cover, what we see is unachievable perfection. I used to compare myself with these images and sometimes compare my life with others, which greatly interfered with my happiness. So I had to find a way to change that.

A flower does not think of competing with
the flower next to it. It just blooms.
—Zen Shin

We all have different talents and agendas. If we take a step back and refrain from being critical and judgmental, we can learn from one another. So all the comparison and competition must be examined, and unhealthy comparison and competition must go. When we feel content with what we have, we don't feel the need to compete.

I decided to compare myself with my past self rather than with others, and I've been pleasantly surprised with some positive changes. Instead of competing with others' successes, I choose to see them as lessons, inspiration, and encouragement. I look for qualities I can emulate and for something that motivates and inspires me to implement them into my life. I look to the examples of love and kindness around me. By introducing these qualities into everyday life, I practice love and nourish myself. They also help me accept and respect other people as they are.

Love Your Age

There is a fountain of youth: it is your mind, your talents, the creativity you bring to your life and the lives of people you love. When you learn to tap this source, you will truly have defeated age.
—Sophia Loren

Some people worship youth and vitality. I prefer to learn the art of healthy living. I can't be young for long. We have youth only for a while, but we can be healthy and beautiful for a lifetime. With a better style of living, I can meet the challenges of growing older. I can change my outlook on health and beauty, live a more colorful and creative life, and accept every stage of life with gratitude. I can add vibrant life to my years. Choosing health and wellness, and embracing aging are game changers. Good health involves peace of mind, trust, and a positive outlook. It's up to me how I live my life. I love the fact that I can change it for the better any time I choose. I can visualize the reality I want, commit to it, and create astounding results in my health and happiness.

Throughout life, we all want to be fit, healthy, beautiful, and age gracefully. It's important to remember that aging isn't about gray hair, wrinkles, or extra pounds. It's about your attitude, vitality, and self-love and acceptance. When you feel young, you look young. Caring more about feeling wonderful most of the time and doing things that make us feel great help create a positive state of mind. Even with gray hair and fine lines, some people just exude youthfulness. Maybe you're one of them or you want to join their club.

For me, the secret of healthy longevity is a holistic approach to life. What enters my body becomes me on emotional and physical levels. The real fountain of youth is a healthy lifestyle. Staying young involves the idea of "everything in moderation" and really taking attentive care of myself, feeling fantastic, and being grateful, creative, and positive. I try to do things that rejuvenate me. When I do activities that enhance my health, they also enhance my life.

A holistic approach can help fortify all the bodily systems. If they're kept in good condition, they'll support wellness and youthfulness. This approach includes positive thinking, nutritious food, healthy beverages, adequate exercise, fresh air, restful sleep, good communication, passion for learning interesting topics, and focus on personal growth and development. As long as we feel engaged with and inspired by life, desired changes will happen. If we maintain a youthful mind full of wonder and curiosity, we'll stay young, healthy, and relaxed.

You may say, "Yes, I understand all that, but I still care about wrinkles." Of course you do. That's normal. But self-love and acceptance can change your outlook. And if you're occupied with interesting assignments, you won't have time to pity or scold yourself.

Your time and energy will be spent wisely, directed in a positive direction, and channeled toward creative work.

In my creative work, I like consistency; it helps maintaining a sense of harmony. And being consistent with good habits is key to feeling younger. The quality of my life depends on such habits and on wise decisions. Every time I make a decision out of love, it improves my life. I try to make choices when I'm in a good mood. When I make a decision based on love, I think it through; I'm not in a rush. I feel both comfort and excitement when I'm happy with a decision. For example, I'm almost done writing my book. What should I do next? What am I curious about? What am I passionate about? What's a consistent step to improve my overall health? I need a project that makes me feel happy and gives my life a rich sense of purpose.

Inspiration involves what excites me. I've always been interested in herbs. In 2006, I took a course and became certified in Herbalism at the Open Center. Unfortunately, I didn't pursue this knowledge then, but I've incorporated some of it into my life. Healing herbs are generous gifts from an abundant earth. The use of herbs promotes vitality and maintains balance in the body. I want to study them thoroughly and apply them to my practice to help others. So my decision has been made based on my passion for herbs. I love the idea of going to school, learning, and meeting new people. Learning keeps me young at heart. I've found a worthy and practical path to follow. I'm happy with my decision. It just feels right.

I believe we can keep ourselves
young by surrounding ourselves with
things that make us feel young.
　　　　　　　　—David DeNotaris

Keeping the mind and body flexible is another secret to maintaining youthfulness. By that I mean a loose attitude that makes it easy to adjust habits and accommodate mental, emotional, and physical changes. This may help you feel better about your health and appearance, and have a better quality of life.

When I redefine my outlook on aging and beauty, I learn more about who I am and become pleased with myself. I can be true to myself.

I turned sixty. I don't mind getting older. I won't fight it. Instead, I want to make peace with it. I just want to look and feel great for my age. I'm not hard on myself, especially when it comes to growing old. I exercise, eat well, and take good care of my mental and physical health. I practice yoga and self-acceptance. To me, aging gracefully means creating healthy discipline around sleeping, eating, and exercising, as well as spending time in nature and with others who are like-minded.

I take no prescription medication. Having peace of mind is my best wellness pill. I use holistic healing methods that empower the body and mind to heal itself. Reflexology is one of them. Also, I use herbal treatments, and I strongly believe in their power. When I want to improve my health, I set a positive intention to deepen my relationship with my mind-body connection. I take time to create an inner sense of calm, treasure time alone, have gratitude for another day, focus on good things in life, and make it as wonderful and magical as I can. Starting each day with gratitude sets the tone and a wonderful atmosphere for the whole day.

For myself, I don't plan to use Botox and other fillers. They seem drastic, aggressive, invasive, painful, and unnecessary. I also like to recognize myself in the mirror. Although when tastefully and skillfully done, with the right amounts, they can be quite enhancing. I've seen people who've had work done who looked really great.

I'm a big believer in facials; I've gotten them regularly since my late twenties. My skin becomes cleaner, plumper, and more hydrated. My face looks radiant with no makeup. My favorite part is the face massage. I always make time for skin care, but I keep my routine simple. I use cleansers, toners, and moisturizers. I also try to get enough beauty sleep, which is a great enhancer of my mood.

We can get the wellness we desire when we make good choices day after day. Set an intention every morning to be better in some way—healthier, wealthier, more confident, more disciplined, more relaxed, kinder, or happier. Make a loving and beautiful change in yourself and build a character you adore from start to finish.

Sometimes we do some work but nothing happens. We don't see any results. This is a time of transformation. The old and familiar must go, so the new and unfamiliar can enter. Keep inspiring and motivating yourself during that time of transformation. Great things happen for people who commit to the process of change.

*Choose to have fun. Fun creates
enjoyment. Enjoyment invites*

*participation. Participation focuses
attention. Attention expands awareness.
Awareness promotes insight. Insight
generates knowledge. Knowledge
facilitates action. Action yields results.*
—Oswald B. Shallow

Love is a way to succeed. Success is a process. It doesn't matter how many steps we need to take toward personal wellness. When we savor each step, we stop counting.

Love Yourself to Compassion

*As I love myself, it's only a short
step to the loving of others.*
—Anne Wilson Schaef

*"If you want others to be happy,
practice compassion. If you want to
be happy, practice compassion."*
—Dalai Lama

Loving myself isn't selfish. On the contrary, the more I learn about my needs, desires, and true nature, the more compassionate and respectful I become toward myself and others. A new appreciation for my own value starts to form, and my priorities change. I begin to love myself with all my flaws, while at the same time working to improve myself, cultivate more compassion, and become kinder and wiser.

What does it take to achieve all that? Loving myself to compassion is really a form of kind and beneficial relationship with myself. I choose to make it as pleasant and caring as possible. By learning more about myself, I can become more empathetic toward others. When I'm interested in my character and in my individuality, I also become more understanding of others. When we treat ourselves well, we treat others well too. A regular practice of compassion makes us feel better and helps us do better.

When I've experienced failure or illness, I've learned how it feels to fail or get sick. I become compassionate toward myself and aware of the challenges of others who go through harsh situations. We all face obstacles, illness, sadness, and failures. We have the same human feelings, needs, goals, aspirations, and struggles. Different situations happen. It's how we handle them that's important. We have different emotional and spiritual paths and traditions, but simple kindness and compassion are universal meeting points.

Compassion is a sympathetic feeling for ourselves and others. It involves the willingness to put ourselves in someone else's shoes and feel empathetic toward that person's feelings to understand his or her pain. It's not always easy to understand others' points of view, feel love for them, and embrace them. It may require us to make an effort to look at issues from a different perspective. We often assume that our opinion is right and the opinions of those who disagree with us are wrong. It's easy to be compassionate toward someone whose life experience and point of view are similar to ours. If a situation is unfamiliar, can we still be compassionate? Yes, we can. We can understand other people's ideas and opinions if we cultivate and practice compassion. It may be a little harder, but we can open our hearts if we choose to.

When life brings hardship, love and compassion can strengthen us. Life isn't perfect, but there are reasons to celebrate and attract more love and compassion into our hearts and days. Love and compassion can improve our ability to remain centered in the face of stress, help us create and enjoy each step forward, and move with a loving pace through all levels of life. They give us the chance to create fresh thoughts, feelings, and actions. They encourage us to keep moving in the direction of our dreams. We can move out of a place of being stuck, being hostile, and being part of a problem, and become part of a solution.

Compassion is something we can develop with practice. We just need the willingness to do so. Learning to practice compassion is simple. When you start criticizing yourself and others, pause and replace your critical and judgmental thoughts with more encouraging and helpful ones. This keeps you connected to your true self.

I've worked hard to gain confidence, self-love, and acceptance. These have come to me gradually, as I've gone through life. I've had a great time developing a sense of love and compassion, and learning to appreciate myself and others.

Whatever life situations we've gone through and whatever intentions we've had, the solution to them all is to be kind, loving, positive, and grateful. The more positive emotions I have, the better equipped I am. When I go mindfully and positively through any life situation, I can master it and produce a positive outcome.

When you're at a point in your life when you don't know what to do or you're lost in terms of health, goals, and choices, you can embark on a journey of loving yourself to compassion and radiant health. Take a walk toward love. Commit to the exceptional and beautiful process of creating wellness. The journey will guide you.

Do you agree that the most important relationship in your life is the relationship with yourself?

CHAPTER 8

General Remarks about a Magical Day

*Each day is a new opportunity. I
choose to make this day a great day.*
—Louise Hay

Make Today Amazing

Hello, morning! I appreciate your beauty. There's magic about a new day. Each one is a miracle and a precious gift. Isn't it wonderful that we can start fresh each morning and make our days more inspiring, useful, interesting, and entertaining.

Loving your everyday life is an art—the art of living healthy, happy, passionately, and positively, and inspiring others to do the same.

Whether I work or have a day off, I treat each day in a special way. Each one has a different energy; some days bring new ideas and enthusiasm. These days flow easily and happily. Other days have a serious, mean, and down energy about them. I realized that accepting the day, whatever its mood is, is the key.

Morning is the best time to set a positive intention for a magical day. When I think positive thoughts, my mind, body, and spirit are in sync. So I wake up every morning and say aloud, "Today I have a feeling that I'll have a wonderful day, and I'll enjoy whatever it brings."

Whatever comes today, I want to be agreeable and make it a priority to feel happy and to feel peaceful about myself and within myself. When I have access to the positive, I can paint the day in bright, vivid colors. Everything seems easy, nice, and enjoyable.

Each day begins the previous evening, with comfortable bed and pillows, a dark and cozy bedroom, and sweet dreams. After a good night's sleep, I wake up refreshed, with pleasant thoughts and words to greet the day. I take a few moments before getting up to think about what I want from the day. I plan each day with a combination of eating well, drinking plenty of water, exercising, completing some accomplishments, and having a sunny attitude toward myself and others. I have a strong intention in creating a favorable day and the determination to be in a light and flexible mood and be generous with anyone I meet on my way—friends, family, coworkers, and strangers.

I used to take days for granted and treated them casually, going through them on autopilot, without noticing the beauty and goodness around me. I admit that I had wasted many days in bitterness, resentment, and disappointment. Sometimes I had even been upset with my days. That was unhealthy and negative, and one day, I said, "I can do better."

Now I'm happy to meet each new day with gratitude. Each one provides its own gifts and opportunities. I'd like to learn to see them and make the most of them. If I meet people who have a sour attitude, there's no need to let them spoil my day. Their mood has nothing to do with me. I don't need their approval. What other people think about me, doesn't influence my attitude. I keep moving, believing in good, and being the best I can be. I'm protected by positive energy, and I'm busy learning how to find meaning and joy in a lovely day.

> *To be calm is the highest*
> *achievement of the self.*
> —Yogi Bhajan

A lot happens each day. How can you end the day with the same energy level you started with? A good piece of advice is this: Don't squander your energy. Rather, spread it evenly. Be selective and wise about where you put your time and attention. If you're upset or in a tough situation or toxic environment, protect your precious power with calmness. You can learn to seal your energy against negative influences. Regardless of what happens, stay calm. Being calm separates you from the environment, and you can enjoy the day. Don't blame or judge others. Let them be the way they are and stay in your own lane. Be happy with what you have today.

When you want to recuperate during the day, chill out for just three minutes. Let your mind, body, and emotions relax by listening to music, taking a nap, reading a book, breathing slowly, or taking a walk. If you want to focus on your goals and dreams, scroll topics of interest on YouTube and choose something you can learn or listen to a medi-

131

tation that relaxes you. When I meditate or read a good article, I'm no longer confronted with the busyness of the day. Such times allow me to rest and replenish my vitality. When I consistently remind myself to be still and calm and pay attention to how I feel, it nourishes my energy and slows down my thinking so I can continue savoring the day.

Another one of my favorite ways to refresh my energy is doing nothing. Each day, I set some time aside to be alone, to be silent, to pause, and to calm myself—my alone time.

During that time of stillness, I listen to myself. I spend time with myself, focus on who I am, and try to connect with myself. I sit in a chair or on a cushion and find a very comfortable position with no music, no phone, and no other distraction. Then I close my eyes. I settle my thoughts and breathe deeply to quiet my mind. Whether I contemplate a picture in my mind that motivates me, reevaluate my desires and what's important in my life, commune with nature, or have a tea ceremony in silence with my thoughts, it helps me learn how to restore my energy.

One-on-one time with myself makes me feel incredible ease and comfort. It's my favorite form of meditation. To me, meditation is the same as relaxation. I'm happy being alone. Quality time with myself creates silence in my mind and helps me set my intentions.

One thing I've learned is not to overwhelm my days. I keep my schedule simple. Two or three tasks a day are all I need to feel productive. I include things like learning to slow down, reducing stress by allowing the day to take its own course and flow naturally, without imposing my ideas or expectations too much and without worrying. I find that when I have a strict idea about how I want a day to go, more often than not, it doesn't go exactly as I had planned. Then I get stressed out, which I can easily avoid if I focus on things that really matter, like working toward my goals and leading a healthy lifestyle. It's much better to be flexible and embrace what comes my way with an open mind. Look at your life and surroundings with positivity and appreciation. Be more present, act with less haste, and trust that each day flows in auspicious and abundant directions.

I've begun seeing my days as an opportunity for service. It's impossible to help and do good for all, but it is possible to help some and do good for some and, most importantly, not harm anyone.

For me, to serve is to approach any situation as a chance to give. There are many ways to give, such as being attentive, caring, appreciative, loving, kind, and respectful.

Listen attentively to yourself, your family, your friends, and others. Give praise, compliments, and encouragement on good strategies, choices, and efforts. We can always lift each other.

Doing good is key to feeling good. The more we give, the more we receive. When we go through the day with good expectations, kindness, gratitude, and giving, we will receive the same. This approach brings us peace, joy, and satisfaction, and also sends these out into the world. The art of giving is the art of developing a good relationship with yourself, nature, and spirituality.

Great-Day Meditation

*An attitude of positive expectation is
the mark of the superior personality.*
—Brian Tracy

One day, I promised myself that I'd learn how to have great expectations for everyday life, since I know that our expectations become reality. As the wise taught, whatever one can visualize, one can achieve. So I committed to training my mind to see the bright side no matter what. I made it a priority to feel good and go through each day in a happy and generous mood. I decided to trust that everything will go well and work in my favor. I get up each morning expecting good things to happen and live my days joyously.

What would you like to create and experience today?

This is a simple and practical technique to help you enjoy the day and improve your mental balance. Find some time to learn and practice it, and you may experience great results.

Notice your thinking, even if it's unpleasant or far from ideal. Don't let it possess you. Just say to yourself, "Oh, how interesting." Be selective about your thoughts. Choose pleasant and encouraging ones. Look for reasons to be happy. Think about what's good in your present situation.

Relax for ten to twenty minutes, then visualize something you want to achieve, create, or improve. Keep your mind on the best and most luxurious things you'd like to do or the person you'd like to be. A dream comes first; then the dream comes true.

Have in your mind a clear picture, a vivid image of yourself and others. Sit down and write exactly what you hope to experience today. Write with a warm and joyful feeling. Keep it to one page; don't go into detail. If a journal is not your thing, you can just visualize your expectation. It's like mentally rehearsing each move of the day.

Have a day with great expectations. Always anticipate success. When you expect something, it will become your experience. The more you're clear and present, the more successful a day you'll have. See your desired vision in your mind and feel it in your emotions as if you already have exactly what you want. Our thoughts and feelings have tremendous power. When we dwell on positive thoughts and good feelings, and act on them, we create a better mood and attitude.

Then simply send an enormous amount of light and love into this scene, until you feel that it's ready to let it go, and watch how it unfolds as the day goes along. When we send good energy into a situation and into the world, it will return to us multiplied.

Don't be attached to a certain outcome. Leave room for the unexpected and the delightful. Let go of things beyond your control. Hope for goodness and, at the same time, be empty of expectations. Just witness and accept what comes your way. When you relax, what you need will come to you. When you approach your day in this open way, you allow the universe to surprise you with something new, different, and even miraculous.

Each person has intuition; they just need to acknowledge it. Listen to your intuition. Trust your inner guidance, and it will help you move in the right direction. When you're attentive to your intuition, it will whisper the right choice, an easy solution. This is the process at work when we've been guided to do something or not do something. I like to listen to these hints and act on them. When I act on them, I realize the benefits of doing so. If we don't honor them, they'll go away. It's a simple way to listen to your inner being, your soul. Don't ignore those whispers.

Intuition visits us every day. Whether we want to take a taxi or the subway, or walk to our desired destination, in our minds, we choose which way to go. When we listen to our intuition, it always leads us to choose the best for us.

Spend more time in a quiet, positive emotional space, and you'll be able to hear better your intuition. When you listen to it, you'll make wise decisions. Favorable situations will present themselves, so be mentally prepared. Tune in to goodness and believe in your dream despite temporary obstacles.

Each day is a chance to start fresh and allow yourself to invite whatever you want into your days. Creating what you want with love, a positive intention and a sincere heart is magical. Extraordinary things happen every day. Take joy in them and make today amazing.

One Day at a Time

In every day, there are 1,440 minutes.
That means we have 1,440 daily
opportunities to make a positive impact.
—Les Brown

I love those days when everything works well and when I get a lot done; people smile and respond very positively, and there's some fun and laughter. I feel good about myself during those days and want to put my mind toward creating more of them.

I've been thinking often lately about how to create one calm and delectable day at a time. Make the future day by day and make each one fantastic. It is doable because we can get help from wise sources, such as tarot cards, horoscopes, numerology, and the *I Ching*.

These systems are like navigational tools that can help us choose a better life direction, know where to focus our attention, and learn how to protect ourselves, especially in turbulent times. They've been popular for millennia because they've been proven to truly assist. They can also satisfy our curiosity about future events. Each of them influences our lives to some degree.

Tarot cards

These can be used to predict the future. If we have a question, we can get an answer from them. Nowadays, it's easy to get a tarot reading on YouTube. I get some of my favorite readings there. Fortune-telling with Tarot cards can be entertaining and very useful.

Horoscope

I also pay attention to the cycles of the moon, and I read my horoscope. It's human nature to be curious about tomorrow. We're under the influence of the planets. The energy of the planets is fascinating and very powerful. It comes into our lives and makes changes, even when we don't ask for it. It comes and goes. It moves all the time, affecting us favorably or unfavorably depending on our moon sign. Our lives depend on the planets' moods. They can rescue us from difficult situations or cause them. There's a lot of mystery around astrology. It's a very interesting topic to learn more about.

Numerology

Another tool for spiritual guidance or life purpose clarity is numerology. Numerology is a mystical arithmetic system that helps us know our character and personality in order to succeed. By listening to a numerologist on YouTube or reading books on this topic, we can educate ourselves and form our own opinions. When we have a dilemma or want direction in a situation or want to learn a new skill, numerology can guide us through the wisdom of numbers. I am amazed by how accurate this information and insight is about my personality, my gifts, my weaknesses, and my talents. It's helped me take positive actions and better understand my personal destiny.

The *I Ching*

This is an ancient Chinese book. *I Ching* means "the system of changes," and it's helped people find meaningful answers to their questions for thousands of years. It's a time-tested method that can assist us in making the right decisions. This book is based on the yin-yang concept, which addresses the idea of change and balance in nature, and inner and outer harmony. The concept of yin-yang originates in the Chinese philosophy of Taoism. Studying this concept helps us lead harmonious and balanced lives. Balance is the heart of ancient Taoist wisdom.

When I consult the *I Ching*, I always see opportunities and learn how to avoid obstacles. I become more aware of the ever-changing conditions around and within me. It's simple, entertaining, and encouraging. After reading an answer to a question, I have an idea what to do or the idea to do nothing or an idea to direct my attention to something else. When I'm confronted with puzzling alternatives, this exceptional book helps me clear my mind and make the right choice. When I make a correct decision based on a feeling of comfort and ease, I can tell immediately because I feel good. I feel a surge of energy and willingness to act on my new plan, as if something's saying, "Your choice was approved."

When I find myself in an unpleasant situation that I can't change, it feels as if some kind of force has lured me into a trap. Of course, it doesn't feel like a trap at first. It usually feels like the right thing to do or say at that time. When time goes by, though, I suddenly realize that it isn't what I thought it was. During difficult times like these, I wonder if I can change my circumstances. Possibly not, but doing healthy and enjoyable activities really helps.

The *I Ching* suggests resting at times like this and cultivating energy for a more favorable future. I always get a good amount of support from the *I Ching*. Its suggestions are helpful. I've learned to embrace this philosophy gladly and calmly because it works well.

Sometimes I interact directly with the universe. I ask a question; then I stop being concerned with it and let it go. When my mind is busy, the answer can't enter. When the mind stops thinking about it, the answer appears. I get it from within or from the cosmos, I'm not sure which. What I know for sure is that each of us has a connection to the universe and its abundance of wisdom. It speaks to us constantly using simple signs. I'm not superstitious, but I try to see the signs.

There was a time when I didn't know how to read the signs that are present every day. I asked my grandmother, a kind and wise woman, about them. I asked her how I should interpret them. I didn't want to miss them. I wanted them to lead my way.

She told me the following story. Imagine yourself walking in the woods. You've walked to the shore of a lake. The lake is still, calm, and beautiful, shining in the sun. You don't see any fish on the surface. How do you know if there are any? Slowly and attentively, look for any signs. You may see a man fishing. That tells you that there are fish.

A sign can be in the form of a phone call, an article in a magazine, a thought out of the blue, a person, a quote, or an overheard conversation. We must pay attention to see them.

Just as using these techniques can help us create wonderful days, learning how to manage our time well will also greatly improve the quality of our lives. I've observed that when I live a fast-paced lifestyle, it's time-consuming and I don't know where my days go.

We all suffer from the conundrum of time. Whether we have a long day at work, get stuck in traffic, or check our emails, our days are busy, and it's hard to carve out time to relax. If you want to spend your time in the very best way and accomplish more, consider its value. It's important to respect time and spend it wisely. Be reverent toward your precious time. Don't let anyone or anything steal your time or energy.

When we respect them, they become our allies and assist us. When we disrespect them, they become our enemies and take revenge on us by withdrawing their power. When I realized that, I became very protective of these valuable assets. I've learned to love being a lady of leisure when I have a few free hours to unwind and revitalize. When I am purposeful, am mindful, and know how to distribute my time and energy well, my days become longer, more productive, calmer, and nicer.

So I established my sweet pace of life. I don't hurry anymore. When I'm late for work or miss my train, I always think, *Everything happens for the best.* I slow down and take time to enjoy each day. Of course, I do what I have to do: work, achieve goals, plan new ones, meet with friends and family, exercise, and lead a healthy lifestyle.

When I want to live my life differently and better, I always try to find what works best for me. A one-day-at-a-time solution works well. By creating a happy day then another happy day, my life starts to consist of beautiful and remarkable days. And yours can too. First weeks, then months. Use your imagination and stimulate your curiosity, and your life can become happy, calm, and enjoyable, despite any situation.

Yes, we can make a delicious day to relish. One day at a time, one step at a time, and one thing at a time. For the time being, I collect wonderful and healthy days in my mind, and I can go there any time I want.

I've learned to value the small joys of every day. No matter our circumstances, we can move forward day by day and plan one day each week to treat ourselves to something special. For me, there's nothing like leaning back in a comfortable chair and reading interesting books or success stories. No offence to Nook and Kindle, but it's one of each day's great pleasures—holding a book and turning the pages while drinking a cup of organic tea. My ideal reading scene is in a cozy coffee shop facing the water. I love creating atmosphere for reading.

Reading has a calming effect and helps me relax. One of my hobbies is collecting interesting books. I own a small but nice library. Some books I can read again and again, and I always find new insights. Developing an interest in classic literature (American, English, French, Russian, etc.) can expand our understanding of life more deeply. It describes different life situations and different people's behavior, and we can learn a lot from it. I believe that relentless learning keeps us young. I love to lose myself in a good book.

I also make a day work for me by setting some time aside to get a facial or foot massage, have a long and pleasant talk with a friend, or just drink a cup of tea alone somewhere to gather my thoughts. It always feels good to take a breather. Sometimes we need to escape into rosy daydreams to regain our energy. When I daydream, it feels like everything is lovely. I call it a playday.

Today I woke up feeling special. I felt so good because I had no schedule for the day. The weather was nice, and I went outside for a long walk by the ocean. During that nice walk, I also enjoyed sitting on a bench drinking hot tea from a thermos. I came back home and put on soft music and had a bubble bath with lavender and herbs.

Then I had a relaxing nap. My gorgeous day of bliss ended with a sumptuous dinner and pleasant conversation with friends at a very classy and elegant French restaurant. I noticed that giving myself such a pleasurable time enlivened my week and had a positive impact on the rest of my life. The best time is when I make time for myself.

I dare to say that my best advice is to allow yourself to do what you want. Please yourself with your favorite activity. Create more time to focus on things that really matter, like laughter, smiles, sun, love, me time, kindness, and gratitude. Find your way to live calmly and happily today and always. When was the last time you gave yourself a day to do exactly what you wanted?

Prioritize Sleep

Early to bed and early to rise makes
a man healthy, wealthy, and wise.
—Benjamin Franklin

A wonderful day starts with sleeping well the night before. Sleep is essential to radiant health, vitality, and beauty. It's the body's natural way of rejuvenating and restoring the brain. When we sleep well, our mind and body repair and renew, which can help our concentration, memory, and mood. This helps us function better and feel our best the next day. Our health and sleep are connected. Adequate, restful sleep is as important to our wellness as good eating and exercise, especially if we want to live a long, healthy, and productive life.

I prioritize my sleep and try to establish a positive relationship with rest and relaxation. I can honestly say that after a good night's sleep, my life is better. I make up my mind more easily, I have a brighter outlook, I focus better, and I feel more alert. In other words, it helps me live more healthfully and happily. When I have enough sleep, I have less stress and better days. It's a big investment in overall health.

If we don't have adequate sleep, we can't function properly. If we don't have quality sleep, our days can be long and exhausting.

An overactive mind, too much excitement late in the evening, too much exhaustion from a long day at work, eating the wrong food, lack of sleep the night before, poor digestion, worry or negative thinking, stress, and drama can all prevent us from sleeping well.

People who have inadequate sleep often become irritable. We need enough time to recuperate from daily anxieties. With better rest, we can prevent serious health issues and gain tremendous benefits for mind and body, like improved immunity and concentration, happier mood, and increased energy. As a bonus, our skin looks fresher and more beautiful, our eyes look brighter and kinder, and we smile more.

I wanted to achieve sound, restorative sleep. I created an elegant, sleep-friendly environment and established a regular relaxing routine before bed. It was a wonderful way to nurture myself and a great way to end the day.

Discover what's going on with your sleep or lack of sleep. Develop your own bedroom routine to reduce stress and enhance your well-being. Making simple, enjoyable changes can help you create a new and healthy habit of drifting off to sleep easily.

Here are some simple and practical tips for a restful night's sleep:

- Write down any worries or plans then forget them.
- Visualize yourself as happy, beautiful, energetic, and successful. Dwell on this vision. Or find another comfortable and pleasant thought and dwell on it.
- Go to bed at the same time each night.
- Get up at the same time each day.
- Train yourself to wake up every day without an alarm clock.
- Eat your last meal of the day about three hours before bedtime. If you get hungry, have a light snack.
- Eliminate alcohol and smoking.
- Keep yourself physically active during the day. For example, take a brisk walk on the way to work or home.
- Get at least twenty minutes of sunlight and fresh air daily.
- Keep your bedroom cool, dark, quiet, and free of technology.
- Make your bed comfortable with cozy linens.
- Block out the world with curtains.

- Take a warm bath or shower an hour before bedtime with lavender and chamomile essential oils to calm a restless mind.
- Burn a lavender-scented candle. Lavender is stress-relieving and makes falling asleep easier; it's soothing, and it calms the mind and emotions.
- Take slow, deep breaths while you're lying down.
- Wear earplugs or play relaxing music.
- Wear a silk eye mask.
- Have a dream pillow (a small sachet filled with aromatic herbs) next to your sleep pillow. Squeeze your dream pillow and inhale the aroma of herbs for a sedative feeling.
- If you want to sleep well, you can also try the following, which support sleeping better: warm milk with honey or valerian, kava, or chamomile tea.

Sometimes I use these herbs, which have relaxing properties, such as valerian or kava. I'm an herb lover. I appreciate side effect-free herbs. They can be especially beneficial for sleep problems. Kava has been used to calm the mind and body, and encourage a good night's sleep. Valerian is my favorite; it's a gentle supplement with a nice taste. It helps me balance my sleep patterns and get enough sleep.

When I realized that sleep is as important as food, water, and feeling good, I began treating it with respect and quality attention. Good sleep is becoming a luxury nowadays. Have that luxury. Let the luxury of sleeping well improve your mood, vitality, health, beauty, and feelings of self-worth. If you want to thrive, you need to prioritize sleep. It's the best medicine. Have a fantastic sleep ritual.

Always retire with a positive thought. Become a master of good beauty rest. Enjoy your sleep tonight and feel more refreshed and energized tomorrow.

My Story

I had a long day at work, and I was tired, maybe even overtired. I felt the need to bring myself into balance, to self-soothe, you could say. I wanted something that would relax and calm me. When negative thoughts and emotional worries occupy my mind, how should I react? The best thing for me to do, is to just write them down, and allow them to be.

When I'm tired or anxious, I go straight to my gratitude journal. I have to be alone with it. Writing in it is a very good form of meditation to help me reflect on the day, especially if it was long and hectic. It plays the role of an attentive psychologist in the comfort of my own home.

Although I don't believe in traditional psychology for myself, I do use reliable information from wise people. I believe I'm full of resources. I have all the tools I need within myself to cope and balance my emotions. I have the ability to become my own therapist and my own support system. My version of therapy is writing in my gratitude journal. I trust and rely on it. Using it is a fascinating process of learning to understand myself better and more deeply.

So I came home, took a warm shower, and put on comfortable pajamas. I wasn't in the mood for dinner. I sat cozy in my bed with a cup of hot chamomile tea with honey and my journal, which provides great emotional support.

In the beginning, I wrote some nonsense, trying to declutter my mind. Then I reviewed my day. Was I harsh on or supportive of anyone? What did I learn today? Have I done anything positive for myself or others? Have I made any mistakes, and if so, do I know how to rectify them? What could I have done differently today? How could I do it better the next time? When I'm satisfied with how my day went, I can relax and have peace of mind and a good night's sleep.

After analyzing my day, all its burdens and negative emotions came to the surface. I wrote them, I talked to them, and I got rid of them. A piece of paper can handle anything. This helped me say goodbye to my inner discomfort and release my inner pain. Tears ran down my cheeks. That was a good indication that I was refreshed. It felt like my journal had absorbed everything bad from me and the day, and let me breathe calmly and peacefully, as if saying to me, "It's gone. Have a pleasant sleep." I felt enormous relief, finished my tea, and had huge appreciation for my journal. It allowed me to acquire a deep and meaningful connection with myself. It can handle all the nonsense without any judgment, letting me be who I am.

That night, I went to sleep on a positive note, relaxed and happy, letting all my worries vanish into thin air and inviting only lovely rest and relaxation. I slept soundly, well comforted by pleasant thoughts. I'm sure I had sweet dreams.

Do you agree it is important for you to develop a good relationship with yourself, nature, and spirituality?

PHYSICAL HEALTH

CHAPTER 9

General Remarks about Food

*Let food be thy medicine and
medicine be thy food.*
—Hippocrates

*By choosing healthy over skinny, you're
choosing self-love over self-judgment.*
—Steve Maraboli

A Well-Balanced Diet

A well-balanced diet is the only way to ensure that the body gets sufficient amounts of the proper nutrients to maintain great and robust health. We are designed to eat the food the earth provides. We can use foods as healing. A simple way of healing is producing balance from within.

We need food, water, sleep, and exercise to achieve equilibrium. Health and happiness are our daily decisions. What we eat, drink, and think all impact our physical and mental well-being.

Having the correct proportion of vitamins, minerals, healthy fats, carbohydrates, proteins, and water helps us boost our energy levels and improve our health the natural way. We rely on food to provide the perfect balance of nutrients for vitality and beauty. Nutrition is a never-ending journey. Like most things in life, it is always a work in progress.

Why don't we make a commitment to work continually toward achieving that perfect balance? Become 100 percent committed to finding the most beneficial foods for your precious health. Choose your food wisely, spend time on menu planning, and see what nutrients you need each day. Variety, moderation, and balance are important considerations. The results depend on us: What we put in, we get out. You and only you are responsible for how you nourish your body. You and only you can determine whether the food you eat results in good or ill health. Let's establish the foundation necessary to create an ideal picture of health. You can start today.

The Basics of a Nutrient-Rich Diet

Eating well is a form of self-respect and self-love. The food we eat affects the way we feel, think, and act. A well-balanced diet supplies us with everything our body needs to be well-nourished and fit. When I choose foods to eat, I always keep in mind what benefits my body can get from them.

There is much conflicting information about food. We can teach ourselves how to make wise food choices. This section shares some simple insights to help you with this process.

People try many diets, and they often don't work. This is because diets are based on theories, and no one theory works for everyone. Every single person is unique and needs a customized approach to food, exercise, and lifestyle. Diet should be based on each individual. There is a formula for each person that applies only to that person. The key is to learn and know this formula. Each person can digest and handle different amounts of different foods. Which foods work best for you, based on your digestion and unique preferences?

We start with basic nourishment. We depend on the main food groups: carbohydrates, proteins, healthy fats, vitamins, and minerals. Each group is a significant component of quality nutrition and is vital for optimal health. Each plays a specific role in proper body nourishment to support a lifetime of good health. Feed your body well.

There Are Two Kinds of Carbohydrates— Simple and Complex

Proper eating is the foundation of overall health. Good nutrition is the process by which the body uses food for energy, growth, and maintenance and repair of body tissues.

Different foods supply us with short-term or long-term energy. Carbohydrates are the main source of energy and the easiest form of energy for the body to use.

1. Simple carbohydrates are mainly sugars. These include table sugar, brown sugar, natural and artificial sweeteners, honey, corn syrup, fruits, fruit juices, sweets,

white bread, cookies, sugary desserts, biscuits, cakes, and milk sugars (ice cream, cheese, milk, and yogurt), and refining and overcooking these have already turned their complex carbohydrates into simple sugars. Simple carbohydrates provide short-term energy, followed by an equally fast drop in energy. After that drop, we want more sugar. These foods don't provide lasting energy. They are useless, antinutrient, and even damaging to optimal health. Stay away from food with refined sugar. Instead of muffins, crackers, bagels, and breads, satisfy your sweet tooth with nuts, seeds, and naturally sweet fresh or dried fruits and vegetables.

When you desire health and wellness, it is extremely important to pay attention to sugar intake. It must be minimized or avoided. Reduce or eliminate the use of simple and processed carbohydrates, such as breads and pasta made with white flour. We should think of processed carbohydrates as hidden sugar in the diet. Occasional use is all right, but in general, one should seek high-quality carbohydrates. For example, when buying items like pasta, seek whole-grain items. They come in countless varieties, each with its own delicious taste and texture. Many stores have a very good selection of both domestic and imported dried pastas, such as quinoa pasta, rice noodles, brown rice pasta, corn pasta (gluten-free), and homemade spaghetti.

Pasta is one of the simplest foods to cook and is loved by almost everyone. It is a smart choice for a healthy diet, especially with lots of vegetables. Experiment with pasta recipes. Fill your refrigerator with sun-dried tomatoes in oil, olives, green onions, fresh basil, parsley, mint, lemons, limes, oranges, sweet peppers, mushrooms, and other fresh foods. Celebrate a wisely chosen pasta with a crisp green salad.

2. Complex carbohydrates or starches. These include whole grains, whole-grain breads, and brown rice; starchy vegetables like potatoes and yams; beans, peas, lentils, and other legumes; and vegetables like broccoli, zucchini, asparagus, cabbage, and turnips. These are your body's best sources of energy. They break down very gradually, release their sugar content slowly, help the body form stool, and leave the system quickly. They require longer digestion to be well absorbed. Complex carbohydrates slow the absorption of sugar and keep blood sugar in balance.

Whole grains are excellent sources of nutrition as they contain essential enzymes, iron, dietary fiber, vitamin E, and vitamin B complex. Because the body absorbs grains slowly, they provide sustained, high-quality energy. Humans have been eating grains for thousands of years. We can choose from a great selection of whole grains, such as oats, quinoa, amaranth, brown rice, bulgur, buckwheat, couscous, millet, rye, wild rice, and barley.

Each grain has it is own benefits. For example, brown rice promotes good digestion and relieves depression. Buckwheat stabilizes blood sugar, normalizes blood pressure, and creates blood. Quinoa strengthens the kidneys, heart, and lungs, and is easy to digest. It is an ideal food for endurance. Grains speed up metabolism and reduce stress. Consider eating them in the morning, as they provide long-lasting energy and a light feeling. Warm and comforting whole grains provide amazing nutritional support.

Incorporate good-quality grains into your diet. They will help you balance your body. Whole grains are some of the most nutritious foods in the world.

I eat grains almost every morning and find myself needing less food during the day. My favorites are buckwheat, brown rice, millet, quinoa, and old-fashioned oats. I dress my grains simply, with ghee (clarified butter) and cinnamon. The fewer ingredients, the better.

Try not to overeat carbohydrates. Cut back on them, from pasta to fruit juice. Consuming excessive amounts promotes body fat. Stop eating before you feel full. Also, the more physically active you are, the more you will burn stored carbohydrates. Switch from highly refined grains to delicious whole grains, which are good and healthy carbs. Balance the amount of complex carbs (one or two servings of vegetables a day and whole grains in moderation).

Fiber

Fiber is essential for the body; we need fiber for healthy digestion. Fiber makes us feel full, keeps the intestinal tract moving, and prevents constipation. Fiber is found in fruits, vegetables, whole grains, and legumes. Good sources of fiber include carrots, broccoli, sweet potatoes, oranges, bananas, oats, prunes, dried apricots, cooked lentils, and sunflower seeds. Fruit should be mostly berries, such as blueberries and blackberries, and pineapples and grapefruits. Tangerines or apples can be added to green salads. Canned fruits and vegetables are loaded with salt and added sugar.

Fresh is better. Frozen fruit and vegetables are nearly as good as fresh ones.

When it comes to vegetables—which are a great source of fiber—it's good to eat many colors and varieties. Painting your plate with the bold colors of orange carrots, yellow squash, purple beets, red tomatoes, emerald-green spinach, and all shades in between makes meals more appealing and also ensures that you get a variety of vitamins and minerals.

Proteins

Proteins are the body's building blocks. Carbohydrates, proteins, and fats are energy-producing nutrients that the body needs to function well. Protein plays an important role in the body, providing all the necessary amino acids. Hair, skin, and bones also contain protein. The body's main organs are all created from protein, and these organs need protein to function properly.

Protein builds new cells, holds cells together, and strengthens the immune system. The body also uses protein to repair, build, and maintain muscle mass. The more muscle we have, the easier it is to burn fat. Our muscles are mostly protein. When protein intake increases, the body forms new muscle. We must maintain the proper amount of protein to have nutritional balance. Fish, poultry, all other meat, eggs, seafood, and dairy products all contain protein.

The amount of protein needed varies from person to person. One must observe the signals of one's body to learn how much protein one needs. It's helpful to keep a food journal and experiment with different forms and amounts of protein at different times to see how you feel in terms of energy, mood, hunger, and mental focus. Personalization is the most important element in the diet. How much protein to eat should be determined by your own body type and digestion. A good general rule is to have portions no larger than the palm of your hand. Some people require a bit of protein with almost every meal. Others do well with mostly vegetarian protein sources like grain and bean combinations or natural soy products and a high-quality animal protein only once or twice a week. And some people feel best with no animal protein. Organic meat is preferable.

Excessive consumption of meat and dairy products contributes to ill health and high cholesterol. When you avoid them, your cholesterol level will drop. You can satisfy your protein cravings with fish or bone broth. There are many types of fish, such as tuna, salmon, shrimp, sardines, mackerel, and anchovies. Use these in salads, wraps, and soups, and as entrées with vegetables.

Small portions of lean meat, such as poultry, seafood, and eggs, can be consumed weekly. Remember the importance of balance and moderation. Choose the best diet with plenty of fiber in the form of raw or lightly steamed vegetables. The vegetables aid the digestion of the meat, and you get the added benefits of fiber.

Eating a variety of fish is healthy and delicious, and it is one of the best ways to meet a daily protein requirement. Fish is preferable to chicken. Wild-caught fish is healthier than farmed fish. A healthy diet with the right amount of proteins will provide you with the building blocks for a fit and strong body.

Seafood

If you like mollusks, such as clams, mussels, or oysters, rinse them thoroughly to remove any sand. Clams, mussels, and oysters can be steamed, baked, grilled, or cooked in soups, stir-fries, or sautés. Put them in a large pot, add water, wine, or beer; fresh herbs, such as cilantro, parsley, or dill; onion; garlic; tomatoes; and green pepper; and let the mixture simmer. Clams and mussels open in about five minutes; oysters in about ten. When your seafood is ready, serve it over whole-grain pasta or rice, garnished with fresh herbs. Add a dash of lemon juice, Tabasco sauce, or your favorite seafood cocktail sauce. Clams provide high amounts of iron, mussels provide essential fatty acids, and oysters provide zinc.

You may also like to try protein-rich crab, shrimp, and lobster. Shrimp are the most popular seafood in the US. They go well with butter, olive oil, fresh herbs, tomatoes, green and yellow peppers, corn, asparagus, and lemon. Shrimp contain high levels of immune-essential minerals, including zinc, selenium, calcium, iodine, magnesium, phosphorous, and potassium, as well as vitamins B_3 and B_{12}.

Eggs

Eggs are truly a whole food, as well as a healthy source of protein. They are easy to digest, and the body can absorb the majority of their protein. Hard-boiled eggs make a great whole food snack. Eggs are a delicious option for any meal.

They can be prepared in different ways, including scrambled, sunny-side up, and in omelets.

Mushrooms

Mushrooms have a long history of use for traditional purposes, both culinary and medicinal. They've been used for thousands of years by the Greeks, Egyptians, and Chinese to promote longevity. Mushrooms have therapeutic properties, such as enhancing immunity, boosting mood, stimulating memory, improving glucose metabolism and digestion, promoting detoxification, and nourishing the body. They also contain fiber, vitamin D, vitamin B complex, antioxidants, and very high-quality digestive enzymes.

Many kinds of mushrooms are available, including white, baby bella, oyster, portobello, shiitake, maitake, and turkey tail. Add mushrooms to a well-balanced diet, especially shiitake mushrooms; they are medicinal, antifungal, and antibacterial. Shiitake mushrooms are versatile for culinary uses. They are low in calories and full of flavor and contain vitamins, minerals, protein, and other beneficial chemicals that help lower cholesterol and make bones sturdier. These tasty mushrooms can be added to meat, pasta, and rice. They make a delicious addition to a vegetable stir-fry or a sauté with garlic and greens. Maitake, like shiitake, are immune boosters. Add warm sautéed maitake to a spinach salad or use them in soups; their firm texture holds up well. Stir-fries are an ideal way to experiment with medicinal mushrooms.

If you are intrigued by the variety of mushrooms in your favorite supermarket, experiment. I love mushroom soup and shiitake pita sandwiches. Delectable mushrooms are a gift that makes us feel good.

Dairy Products

Good cheese is derived from good milk. Isn't it incredible that people have come up with more than a hundred types of cheese perfectly classified by taste, texture, and flavor? It's great that we can benefit from their talented and exquisite work. However, overconsumption of dairy promotes mucus production and indigestion. Excessive mucus doesn't let us absorb nutrients. As we age, we don't need as much dairy. Our bodily enzymes also change as we age, so bloating and gas may be produced.

Calcium also comes in healthy alternatives, such as dark green leafy vegetables, broccoli, beans, nuts, and seeds.

Many stores have an impressive selection of cheeses. My favorites include goat cheese, farmers cheese, baby swiss cheese, cream cheese, brie, and mozzarella. I don't deprive myself of these tasty foods. I just enjoy them in moderation. I used to keep a journal to explore foods. It helped me tremendously. I've experimented with different foods and made my happy choices a long time ago by carefully selecting food that agrees with me. They are light and delicious. I made room in my life for special cheeses, consumed only occasionally in small portions.

Farmer cheese can be eaten alone or in salads. Cream cheese can be used in sandwiches. Mozzarella is often used in salads or marinated for an appetizer. Brie is delicious with crackers, bread, or fruit for desert. A plate of cheese, thinly sliced green apple, and grapes is always a wonderful idea when you want to celebrate.

Cheese is savory, while green apple and grapes are juicy and sweet. Have your own happy hour: a snack like this can be a highlight of the day. Take yourself on a journey of cheese experimentation. Become a cheese connoisseur in a healthy and nutritious way.

Legumes

The legume family includes beans, peas, and lentils. Legumes have plenty of fiber and are a wonderful way to add high-quality plant-based protein and carbohydrates to your diet. They also contain vitamins and minerals. There are many legumes to choose from, such as adzuki beans, Anasazi beans, black (turtle) beans, cranberry beans, garbanzos (chickpeas), great northern beans, kidney beans, lima beans, mung beans, navy beans, pinto beans, soybeans, black-eyed peas, split peas, and lentils (brown, green, red, and yellow). Legumes are versatile enough that you may never tire of them. Beans stay fresh longer when stored in a cool, dark place. Don't use beans that are more than a year old, as their nutrient content and digestibility are much lower.

Chew beans thoroughly and know that even small amounts have high nutritional and healing value. Experiment with your ability to digest beans. Smaller legumes such as adzuki and mung beans, peas, and lentils are more easily digested. Black beans, garbanzos, kidney beans, lima beans, navy beans, pinto beans, and black-eyed peas may be harder to digest and should be eaten only occasionally. Soybeans are the most difficult legumes to digest.

Try different combinations, ingredients, and seasonings. Legumes combine best with green or nonstarchy vegetables and seaweed. Combinations of grains and legumes (such as beans or peas with rice) are delightful. Legumes can take the place of meat as a main course. They can be dressed with nothing more than a little olive oil and a splash of lemon juice. One serving of legumes each day can be a primary protein source. Many people do well with vegetarian protein sources.

Season your beans with unrefined sea salt, miso, or soy sauce near the end of cooking. If added at the beginning, the beans will not cook completely. Salt is a digestion aid when used correctly. Adding fennel or cumin near the end of cooking helps prevent gas.

Pour a little vinegar (apple cider, brown rice, or white wine types) into the water in the last stages of cooking. This softens the beans and breaks down proteins and indigestible compounds, which can prevent bloating.

I eat lentils pretty often—they're easy to use and cook quickly. I add lentils to soup, toss them in salads, and stir them into my favorite cooked rice. Which beans do you choose?

Fats and Oils

Invite omega-3 essential fatty acids into your diet. They are good for your heart, brain, skin, weight, and overall health. Like carbohydrates, fats and fatty acids are energy providers. Fats also play an essential role in a balanced diet. Our brains are 60 percent composed of fat or, more specifically, fatty acids. They are essential for healthy brain cells. Fat protects our central nervous system. Good fats prevent the accumulation of cholesterol in our arteries, build strong cells, strengthen artery walls, and help create necessary hormones. Fat from high-quality oils and whole foods is used by our bodies to help keep our metabolism steady and nourish our skin, hair, and nails. We should make sure to get adequate healthy fats, such as flaxseed oil and fish oil. We need good fats to absorb vitamins A, C, and E. However, overconsumption of fat leads to obesity. Too much of anything is unhealthy.

Healthy fats include extra-virgin olive oil, coconut oil, unrefined sesame oil, ghee (clarified butter), whole nuts and seeds, nut butters, whole food fats from avocados and coconuts, and high-quality oil in cold-water fish, such as salmon and tuna. All fish are high in protein and low in saturated fat. Oily fish, such as Alaskan salmon, Alaskan black cod, and canned sardines, provide omega-3 fatty acids. Enjoy baked, grilled, or steamed fish three times a week for delicious healthy fats.

For sautéing and baking at high temperatures, use ghee or coconut oil (old-fashioned products) because they do not break down under extreme heat. When sautéing and stovetop cooking at moderate temperatures, try ghee. Ghee lowers cholesterol and is rich in vitamins A, D, and K. Try ghee on steamed broccoli and potatoes.

Nut and seed oils, such as toasted sesame oil, flaxseed oil, walnut oil, pumpkin seed oil, and almond oil, are best used unheated. Cold-pressed unrefined oils are the best types. They are the healthiest types of fats. They can be used freely in salad dressings. Drizzle them on salads, veggies, or grains just before serving. Never heat flaxseed oil or toasted sesame oil, as this destroys nutrients. Sesame oil is healthy and tastes great.

Extra-virgin olive oil is my favorite. It has benefits for your skin, heart, blood pressure, and mental well-being. Try a piece of whole-grain bread or crackers topped with olive oil. Add sliced garlic or onion, cucumber, tomato, and arugula, and sprinkle with sea salt and pepper. This tastes great as a snack or small dinner.

Cut down on saturated fats, which are derived from meat, vegetables, and dairy products, such as butter, milk, and cream. I keep it simple: a tablespoon of flaxseed or fish oil in the morning, olive oil with a salad, and ghee for cooking.

Healthy fats and oils, whether found in foods or used in cooking, are an important source of fuel in a well-balanced diet. Our bodies need fat to insulate us, keep us warm, protect our organs, and hold them in place. Fat plays a complex role in our health. It improves overall organ function and keeps our brains sharp. Experiment with fabulous fats and oils. Everything in moderation: the golden rule.

Green Vegetables

A well-balanced diet of healthy foods has the exact right combination of nutrients for each individual's body. Vitamins and minerals are essential for maintaining the body's metabolic function. It's better to get them from food than from pills. Fruit and vegetables are rich in vitamins and minerals. We need one serving of fruit and two of vegetables per day. The body needs vitamins for growth, maintenance, and repair.

Minerals must be obtained from a well-balanced diet for better bones, teeth, and cells. On most days, try to eat at least one serving of dark green leafy vegetables. These vegetables are the most important vegetables to incorporate daily. Nutritionally, greens are very high in calcium, magnesium, iron, and vitamins A, C, E, and K. They are crammed with fiber, folic acid, and many other micronutrients.

Some of the benefits from eating greens are as follows:

- Blood purification
- Improved circulation
- Cancer prevention
- Strengthened immune system
- Promotion of healthy intestinal flora
- Improved liver, gallbladder, and kidney function
- Lifted spirit

You can find a great variety of greens, such as arugula, bok choy, broccoli rabe, chicory, collards, dandelion, kale, lettuce, mustard greens, spinach, and watercress. You can start eating some greens this week. Be adventurous and try glorious greens that you've never heard of before. Choose one or two new greens and experiment. Find greens that you love and eat them often.

Arugula contains more calcium than kale and collards—two greens noted for their high calcium content. Arugula also adds flavor and visual appeal to your meals. It can be used with pasta, soups, potato dishes, salads, and sandwiches. It's delicious when served with dressings made with citrus juices and vinegars.

Try a variety of cooking methods, such as steaming, boiling, and sautéing in ghee, coconut oil, or water. Cooking damages or destroys some important nutrients. Vitamin C and folic acid, for example, are sensitive to heat. Boil for under a minute so that the nutrients in the greens do not leach into the water. Boiling makes greens plump and relaxed. You can also drink the cooking water as a health-giving broth if you're using organic greens. Raw salad is also a wonderful preparation for greens. When you nourish yourself with greens, you'll crowd out less nutritious foods.

Learning to cook and eating greens is essential to creating health. Get into the habit of adding dark green leafy vegetables to your daily diet. Try them for a month or more and see how you feel.

Take simple but effective steps to upgrade your health. It just requires a little organization. Only you know when to push hard and when to ease up. Enjoy every meal of the day.

Sea Vegetables

Sea vegetables are high in calcium, iron, potassium, magnesium, zinc, iodine, and vitamins A and B complex, including B_{12}. They are alkaline and nutritious; and they have calming and soothing effects on the health, mood, and personality. Many varieties are available, such as arame, dulse, hijiki, kelp, kombu, nori, and wakame. They each have different flavors, so experiment and include them in your meals as often as you like.

Seaweed is low in calories and high in fiber, and provides a large percentage of the minerals your body needs daily. It also improves digestion and strengthens bones and teeth.

Wakame is a sweet, delicious, nourishing sea vegetable traditionally used in Chinese medicine to purify the blood and strengthen the intestines, skin, and hair. It's the seaweed usually added to miso soup. Preparation is simple. Soak it in cold water for five minutes. Rinse, slice, and use in soups, stews, vegetable dishes, and salads.

Kelp is high in calcium and iodine. It can be used as a salt substitute or powdered condiment.

Nori is the seaweed used to wrap sushi. It comes in paper-thin sheets, and it is crispy when lightly toasted. I use nori often, especially when I need a delicious meal idea for a light dinner. I like either cooked brown rice wrapped in a sheet of nori, with a dash of tamari (soy sauce) or steamed broccoli wrapped in nori.

Sweet Vegetables

Satisfy your sweet tooth by adding sweet vegetables to your meals. They are low calorie, tasty, and packed with antioxidants.

For a deep, sweet flavor when cooked, try beets, carrots, corn, onions, winter squash (such as buttercup, butternut, and delicata), sweet potatoes, and yams. Sweet potatoes are a good source of vitamins A, C, E, and B_6, and are high in potassium, folic acid, and fiber. They're available year-round, and their peak season is September through January. Sweet potatoes are among the oldest vegetables. For a subtle sweetness, try parsnips and turnips.

Certain vegetables don't taste sweet, but the effect on the body is similar to that of sweet vegetables. Try burdock, cabbage (red and green), daikon radish, and red radish. These vegetables help keep blood sugar levels even and break down old animal foods in the body.

When you cook sweet vegetables, you can add spices, salt, and seaweed. You can add tofu or some beans for extra protein. Cooked sweet vegetables help appease your sweet tooth and help fight sugar cravings.

Experiment with a variety of sweet vegetables. Choose your favorites and have a good range of nutrients in your diet. The nutritional benefits and natural sweetness of these vegetables can inspire you to put them on your table often.

My Story

Some people can avoid sugary things or can eat them in moderation, and I wanted to associate with them. I told myself that if they can do that, I can too.

I tuned in to my body and mind, got motivated, got an agreement with myself, and declared that I was going to make peace with sugar. I had a strong belief that I was going to do it. The more tuned in I was, the easier it was to make adjustments to stay on the right track.

I kept a food record as I made positive and lasting dietary changes. I was adding food rather than taking food away. My strategy was to include naturally sweet healthy foods, such as carrots, sweet potatoes, and peppers, to my everyday eating so that they'd push out unhealthy foods. My first step was to cut my sugar intake in half for one week. The next week, I cut it in half again. After three weeks, I no longer craved sweets. Once I did this, my diet became low in sugar, and I was able to have sweet treats occasionally with no discomfort. When I make changes, I try to be kind and gentle with myself.

I usually had sugar cravings around 4:00 p.m. to 5:00 p.m. So I prepared for that time period with good alternatives, such as naturally sweet fruit and vegetables. However, to my surprise, I didn't have as strong a desire for sweets as I'd thought I would.

This approach helped me remove most sugar from my diet gradually and permanently. I've noticed that I'm more productive than before and my focus and clarity have improved.

By adopting a sensible no-sugar or very-low-sugar eating plan for life, we can achieve our ideal weight and enjoy robust health. What we do today for our health will impact us in the future. The less sugar we eat, the better our bodies function. We always get to create what we want.

The body needs each of the basic food groups, which ensures that we get all the necessary nutrients. Each food group plays a different role in bodily nourishment. When we stick to mainly whole grains, legumes, nuts, seeds, lean meat (including fish), fruits, and vegetables, our health gets better. Our hair, skin, and nails become beautiful; our digestion improves naturally; and our energy level is enhanced. We become filled with vitality, and most importantly, we feel great.

Do you agree that the food you eat results in overall health?

CHAPTER 10

General Remarks about Beverages

*Drink your tea slowly and reverently, as
if it is the axis on which the world earth
revolves—slowly, evenly, without rushing
toward the future. Live the actual moment.*
Only this moment is life.
—Thich Nat Hahn

Liquid Goodness

Water, coffee, tea, and juices are beverages that enhance
our beautiful journey through life toward radiant health.
Drink your way to wellness. Keep your energy moving and
feel super.

Water

Water is very important. It's our most effective elixir.
It's a vital ingredient for the healthy functioning of all the
body's systems. This cannot be overstated. We can survive

for only a few days without it. We're also made of mostly water; it makes up 80 percent of the body.

In Chinese philosophy, the water element organs are the kidneys and bladder. These organs govern metabolism. The kidneys remove waste products from the body and keep both the body's chemicals and its water at their proper levels. They also clean our blood. In addition, the kidneys are seen as the root and foundation of the body. They also provide energy and warmth. Weak kidneys generate fearful feelings. People with healthy kidneys are active, calm, courageous, and gentle. Plenty of water and proper nutrition are needed for building the vital essence of the kidneys. Without this essence, old age occurs rapidly. Flush all internal organs (kidneys, gallbladder, and colon) and blood daily with good-quality water. This promotes good digestion and healthy skin with a beautiful complexion; improves concentration, circulation, and vitality; and hydrates cells so they can function at high levels.

Develop a good hydration habit. Drink an adequate amount of plain water. Water has a gentle natural diuretic effect. Drinking six to eight glasses of pure water daily helps kidneys do their job well. Start your day with a glass or two of room-temperature water, which is better for digestion than ice-cold water. Plain water is best. It should be filtered and should not be kept in a plastic bottle. Go with what tastes good to you and drink as much water you need. Sometimes we think we're hungry when we're really thirsty.

We don't need special water with vitamins or herbs. Flavored water tends to be full of sugar, artificial sweeteners, and other additives. I sometimes like to add two tablespoons of molasses to a glass of water. Molasses is a significant source of iron, calcium, and potassium.

It's best to have most of your water intake during the morning and afternoon. This can help you sleep through the night without interruption. Drinking water thirty minutes to one hour before and after meals is ideal for good digestion. Drinking too much liquid during a meal dilutes digestive enzymes and stomach acid, which we need for optimal food digestion. Other beverages, such as tea, coffee, and juices, don't replace the need to drink plain water, just as vitamins and minerals don't replace the need for food.

Coffee

Nowadays we can try hundreds of coffees from around the world, such as Arabica, Colombian, Turkish, and Italian. Coffee provides a bitter flavor that our taste buds desire. Drink the highest-quality coffee you can obtain. Try to buy 100 percent organic. It's also best to buy whole coffee beans and grind them just prior to use or buy small amounts of freshly ground coffee. If buying decaffeinated coffee, look for steam- or water-processed. Herbal coffees are also available. Some kinds contain no actual coffee. They tend to contain roasted soy, barley, or chicory, and sometimes combined with other herbs and spices.

Coffee drinking has been linked to better energy and feel-good emotions. I count myself among coffee lovers. When I can smell, taste, and relish the aroma of coffee, I feel uplifted and happy. Sipping a delicious coffee in the morning is like a meditation or a pleasant ritual for me. I dream over coffee. I take five extra minutes to set my desired and positive intentions for the day. This is my secret for a better morning. I'm truly ready for anything that comes my way. It sets me on the path to making healthy choices for the rest of the day. I take my coffee black with a slice of lemon and perk it up with a sprinkle of cardamom or cinnamon.

A little coffee ritual to greet a new day is a pleasant event. Getting a lovely cup of coffee creates bliss. Sip your coffee your way for enjoyment. Stay lively and upbeat.

Tea

Although I prefer herbal teas, I occasionally drink loose black tea. Due to its caffeine, it gives me an energy boost, and I also love the flavor. I like to drink it in a crystal glass so I can admire its beauty.

Think of herbal teas as natural remedies. Why not start sipping and savoring medicinal teas?

- Teas that can aid digestion: teas containing ginger, fennel, peppermint, licorice, cardamom, cinnamon, clove, dandelion, raspberry, blackberry, violet, and watercress.
- Teas that can aid in relaxation and stress reduction: teas with kava kava, chamomile, Saint-John's-wort, catnip, lavender, lemon balm, valerian, and yarrow.
- Teas that can boost energy: green tea, ginseng, and black tea.
- Teas that can enhance immunity: teas with echinacea and goldenseal, and green teas.

- Teas that can help prevent and cure colds and flu: teas with angelica, elderberry, ginger, and marshmallow.

Green tea has been popular in China and other Asian countries for thousands of years. It has many health benefits. It is anti-inflammatory, lowers blood cholesterol levels, has a beneficial effect on circulation and liver, protects against tooth decay, detoxifies the blood, and is an excellent immune-system booster. It's been recognized for its medicinal aspects for more than four thousand years. For maximum benefit, let it brew for at least five minutes. Some teas need to steep for more than ten minutes to gain their full effects, while others need just a few minutes, so look on the box for ideal steeping times. Organic loose tea is the optimum choice, although tea bags are quite convenient. White tea also invites our attention with its delicate flavor. It also has anti-inflammatory and germ-killing properties.

Winter or summer, I like my tea warm. Even on a very hot summer day, I enjoy hot lavender green tea. However, cold green tea is also an ideal thirst quencher. Whether you take your tea hot or cold, have some quiet and quality time for yourself every day to relish your favorite tea. Create a feeling of calm and equilibrium.

Green mint tea

2 tbsp. green tea
4 c. boiling water
Large bunch of fresh mint
Brown sugar or honey to taste

Place the tea in a teapot and cover it with boiling water. Let it steep for 3 minutes. Wash the mint. Reserve a few sprigs for garnishing; then add the rest to the pot, and leave for 5 minutes. Pour into glasses, adding sweetener if desired. Garnish with the reserved sprigs of mint.

Drinking herbal teas is one of the simplest and most effective and pleasurable ways of using natural herbal remedies. They help nourish the body and mind. I'm a big lover of herbal teas with medicinal properties and truly believe in herbal medicine. These teas can offer relief from many discomforts, such as colds, flu, and headaches. They are made from dried herbs, flowers, and fruits. As with everything, they should be used in moderation. I buy teas loose at health food stores. I usually alternate between water, juices, and teas throughout the day. I include a few cups of herbal tea in my everyday routine.

Some of my favorite herbal teas are ginkgo biloba, ginger, licorice, Korean ginseng, and chamomile.

Ginkgo biloba tea has a delicate flavor. It improves blood flow through the arteries to the brain, alleviating vertigo, headaches, depression, poor concentration, and other age-related disorders. It can help prevent strokes and heart attacks, slow the aging process, and improve memory. It can also help eyes, ears, and legs function better.

Ginger root aids in digestion and stimulates appetite. It can help fight colds and flu, bring down a fever (hot ginger tea is helpful with perspiration), activate immunity, remove mucus, boost blood circulation, and help warm the body, especially in cold weather. Slice or grate fresh ginger and simmer in water for ten to fifteen minutes. Sip hot or cold.

Ginger tea

3 to 4 tsp. chopped fresh ginger root
1 tsp. licorice root (optional)

Place ginger root and 2 cups of water in a small pot. Bring the water to a boil, cover the pan, turn down the heat, and simmer over low heat for 10 to 15 minutes. Strain out the herbs and discard them. If you don't use licorice root, sweeten the tea with honey.

Licorice helps restore the adrenal glands, benefits the endocrine system, and increases estrogen. It also relieves respiratory discomfort from a cold, bronchitis, or a cough, and is soothing for sore throats.

Korean ginseng improves vitality, strengthens the immune system, balances the hormones, and relieves fatigue and depression.

Chamomile flowers have soothing and calming properties. Chamomile tea calms digestive upsets, relaxes the nervous system, and promotes restful sleep. It's also useful for anxiety and insomnia.

I consider herbs wise supplements for radiant health. I love them all. Experiment to see what works for you. Savor freshly brewed high-quality herbal tea.

I believe in tea therapy. Create a ceremony for yourself that can act to quiet your mind and help you relax.

Juices

Drinking fresh juices changes the way we feel. Freshly squeezed fruit and vegetable juices are a great source of vitamins and minerals. They assimilate quickly, taking only fifteen minutes for the body to digest. Raw fruit and vegetable juices provide healing properties for the body and enhance digestion. They can also improve sleep, build immunity, and provide a lifetime of health benefits.

It is easy to make freshly squeezed juices. Buy the highest-quality produce you can afford and a good juicer. Invest in a juice extractor that lets you experiment with different fruits and vegetables. By blending small amounts of juice, you can find combinations that suit your taste. You can combine vegetables and fruit. My favorite is carrot and apple juice. As with herbs, I consider fresh juices wise supplements.

My Story

Years ago, I was diagnosed with anemia (iron deficiency). I was often tired, had cold hands and feet, and had dizziness, which are common symptoms of anemia. All these symptoms kept me from enjoying life fully. At first, I got scared and depressed, but then I realized that depression was not a strategy. I had to pull myself together and do something about it. Instead of sinking into my sadness, I envisioned my desired health and decided to take on the project of falling in love with myself. I was strongly motivated to regain my energy and vitality and to enjoy myself and everyday life. I told myself that I'd return to true health for good. Because of my desire to do that, I had enough perseverance and self-discipline to make it happen. My body sent me a signal in the form of anemia to direct my attention to improving my health naturally.

I started my own healing process. I took steps to keep my body robust and my mind positive. I visited my local library for inspirational and nutritional books and magazines to get my creativity flowing. I researched a healthy diet. My target was to find highly beneficial foods, especially foods high in iron, that nourish the body well and that would create a balance between proteins, carbohydrates, healthy fats, and lots of fruit and vegetables. I had consumed all available information on the topic of nutrition. I found many contradictions, too, but that didn't stop me. I felt compelled to continue my search for my own truth, my own nutritious, my delicious eating style, and my own rules about what makes me feel good and healthy.

I wasn't looking for a quick fix; instead, I wanted to give my body a chance to heal itself. Bodily healing happens over time when provided with proper nutrition and positive thinking. I listed all the things I could do for myself to improve my health and lifestyle. The list was pretty long, but I enjoyed my own recommendations and truly believed in them. Each day, I nourished myself with love, undivided attention to my precious well-being, and nutritionally rich foods, especially freshly squeezed vegetable juices. I began drinking fresh juices (carrot, apple, greens, lemon, and grapefruit) and ginger tea, and getting fresh air, good sleep, rest, relaxation, and gentle exercise (walking). These gave me a huge dose of optimism on a regular basis. In addition to my juice therapy, I enjoyed drinking smoothies made with fruit or greens. Sometimes these could replace one or two meals a day.

Three months later, I had achieved positive results. I felt better, and my energy level had increased. I began to study yoga and go to the gym. Since that time, nutrition and wellness were a hobby of mine for years, and later, the hobby turned into a profession I love.

Even though I had a health scare, looking back on it, I can say that it was therapeutic, interesting, self-enriching, and even uplifting. I realized that there was a part of my life that had been put on hold. When a health issue appeared, it gave me a strong push, showing that it deserved my undivided attention. When illness happens, out of panic, we can change our approach to wellness. Our old excuses about lack of time and money disappear. We can shift our focus and put ourselves first if we hit the reset button and start again. But we can also achieve our goals with love and appreciation rather than out of panic and depression.

During this healing process, I learned a lot about myself. I discovered new sides of myself. I learned some new and beneficial habits. I did what was necessary for my strong health. I was able to recover, achieve and maintain balance, and ensure success in living healthfully. This learning process enabled me to develop the best diet for myself and a lifestyle filled with joy and energy. This experience taught me a very good and valuable lesson, which is to never neglect your health and never take it for granted. Always keep a close eye on wellness and treat it with reverence. My well-being is now my number-one priority. I try to live a life of total health. I take pleasure in making an exceptional commitment to myself and my future.

In the middle of my new and wonderful routine, I became interested in holistic health, which emphasizes disease prevention. Disease prevention should be primary and treatment secondary. I believe that if it's treated early enough, there's no such a thing as an incurable health condition. Any health concern can be changed at least 90 percent, and possibly cured, with the right diet, lifestyle, and attitude. Such conditions are often caused by particular lifestyles, and lifestyles can be improved.

Do you drink healthy beverages your way to wellness?

CHAPTER 11

General Remarks about an Inspiration

*It is always the simple that
produces the marvelous.*
—Amelia Barr

One Must Have an Inspiration

What inspires you to eat well and stay healthy? While I'm completely inspired to be healthy, I still need a good, strong inspiration to create a well-balanced eating routine and a healthy and optimal lifestyle. After inspiration comes sustainable motivation and the willingness to do something beneficial for myself. Motivation is a lasting source of good energy. When motivation is at hand, it takes me straight to wellness.

Being inspired means having the creative energy to achieve any health goal. When you're excited about something, you have enthusiasm and vigor. When I invest time and energy creating true health and noticing how it makes me see things in a new light, true health eventually displays itself. A good inspiration is a solid foundation for new beginnings. It pulls you forward and may even entice you to adopt creative ways to live healthfully.

I keep my inspiration alive by surrounding myself with lovely motivators. They remind me to keep my health a top priority. A motivator can be a picture, a note, or a quote. I keep a personal promise and a picture of a beautifully fit woman on my refrigerator. I keep my gratitude journal open with an inspiring quote or a note stuck to my mirror that says, "You are doing famously great! Keep it up!" Motivation gives me the energy to be consistent, to be present, to be prepared, and, of course, to be happy. To get motivated to work out, I just talk to myself. I tell myself, "Darling, you will feel so much better mentally and physically after you go for a walk or work out."

How to find inspiration? It's around you everywhere. Just think about people who positively influence your life. What qualities do you admire about champions, mentors, actors, and role models? What steps can you take to nurture these qualities in your daily life? We can see very successful people all around us, and we can be motivated by their success.

Just engage your curiosity and imagination, and find your true inspiration. When you have a vision for your health, beauty, and confidence, and when you're ready to become the person you want to be and live your life differently and better, inspiration will present itself to you when you least expect it. Even little inspirational episodes from everyday life can turn into an enjoyable process toward wellness. I've found inspiration in different cultures and in traveling. I love taking photos of beautiful places and different types of design and fashion. Everywhere I go, I look for inspiration. I draw my daily dose from my role models as well.

I have a role model for every aspect of my life. They keep me busy and make my life exciting. When it comes to health and energy, I like reading self-help books, health magazines, and yoga journals. I want to maintain my body and have good overall health. I'm eager to learn from other people's perspectives and experiences, and incorporate beneficial tips into my everyday life.

When it comes to beauty and style, I adore Grace Kelly's elegance. I take pleasure in fashion. I don't follow fashion blindly; I prefer to keep my own style, but I like browsing shiny, colorful glamour magazines. It's a great way to discover new fashion ideas and include them in a casual everyday look. I gladly embrace new and lovely seasonal elements. By having my own style, which I think is casually elegant, it's easy to follow any fashion.

When it comes to courage, strength, perseverance, and determination, I turn to the power of positive thinking. It interests me, keeps me in a positive mood, helps me acquire knowledge, and teaches me how to make good use of it. My role models inspire, motivate, assist, encourage, and support me through life. I have deep appreciation for them.

Another priority is training myself to always stay in a good mood and learning simple, interesting ideas to better the quality of my life. I read for enjoyment and inspiration, commune with nature and myself, and take different courses on self-enrichment. The best investment I can make is learning how to have an open mind and peace of mind.

Take very good care of yourself. Have vitality, stay healthy, dress nicely, look enticing, and pamper and love yourself. Celebrate your progress and become the best version of your inner contentment. A wonderful life is ahead of you. Be healthy, energetic, intelligent, beautiful, and fabulous.

My Story

It was winter, and the weather was cold and snowy. It was my birthday celebration dinner with my close friends and family. We went to one of my favorite french restaurants, the River Café, which has a magnificent view of Manhattan. We had a nice table by the window. It was a perfect spot. We enjoyed the lights of the city and the beauty of the Hudson River.

The white tablecloths, the candles, the flowers, the lighting, the piano music, and the ambiance were exquisite and special. The restaurant was cozy and inviting. We even forgot about the cold weather. We were surrounded by a magical atmosphere.

Everyone was happy, beautiful, and dressed up. I wore a black dress, high-heeled boots, a pearl necklace and earrings, and a smile of happiness. Everything was to my liking and to my taste.

We had drinks, appetizers, the first course, the second course, and so on. The presentation of the food was a work of art. The portions were small but just the right size to satisfy my appetite. I prefer quality food over quantity. The meal was delicious. It made me want to savor each bite. I saw lovely familiar faces. We had a wonderful time in harmonious surroundings, enjoying each other's company and conversation. It was pleasant and uplifting.

It was time for dessert. I had a Brooklyn Bridge chocolate cake with a birthday candle on top to make a wish. I looked around, and something made me pause. A perfectly designed restaurant and garnished meals and breathtaking view. I was hugely inspired by the beauty of the evening. It captured all my favorite moments. My wish was to get to know the food and everything associated with it better, create my own healthy eating style, and turn my kitchen into a palace of elegance and minimalism (buying only what I need). I wanted to go home and create something similar and treat my mealtimes in a special and beautiful way.

I was eager to have my wish and kept thinking of benefits. I spent the entire next day making my wish come true. I even forgot to eat because I was so engaged in the process, creating a whole-grain shelf, a condiment shelf, a herb shelf, a coffee and tea zone, and a napkin corner.

That day was awesome. It was the beginning of my new, healthy, and nutritious eating style. I felt happy and inspired to act toward my radiant health and beauty. I appreciate my inspiration and my efforts because they assisted me in getting where I wanted to go. What a power of inspiration. Inspiration does work. I would call it a primary food.

Primary foods are really the first source of energy. They don't come on a plate. They're things that feed and nourish our souls, such as a passionate project, a satisfying career, a good relationship, a spiritual practice, and regular exercise. When you're so involved in an interesting and exciting project that you forget to eat, you're filled with love, creativity, enthusiasm, and excitement. These feed you well, and nutrition becomes a secondary source of energy.

I'm sure you've noticed when you're in a good mood and feeling happy and joyful because of an interesting activity you anticipate or are participating in. You're filled with light, excitement, and productive energy. At that moment, your primary food is balanced and fulfilled. The more primary food we receive in the form of satisfying work and hobbies, yoga and meditation, and pleasant conversations with friends and family, the less we are dependent on secondary food. Secondary food satisfies our physical hunger, while primary food satisfies our emotional hunger. When primary food is abundant, it feels awesome. What is your passion project?

Eating for Vitality and Beauty

The food you eat is reflected in the mirror—your eating choices affect how you look and feel. Whether you like your image or not, there's always room for improvement. Try to simplify your food consumption. Opt for the best food choices for your precious health and beauty.

A well-balanced diet, a nutrient-rich diet, and the Mediterranean diet seem the same. The Mediterranean diet is good for us and is centered on foods that most of us love. It's also practical and easy to follow. It's based on olive oil, wine, and other important ingredients, such as whole grains, legumes, pasta, garlic, greens, cheese, meat (including fish), eggs, fruit, and lots of vegetables. I consider all these appealing foods medicinal and healing, when eaten in moderation, of course. Medicinal food helps the body heal itself and maintains balance, as well as being delicious and nutritious.

Luckily, most foods are available to us year-round. We also have access to food from all over the world. It doesn't matter what you call your diet. Just build a healthy base by making sensible food choices each day. Time spent choosing food wisely is time invested in wellness. Fueling yourself with nutritious and filling foods first thing in the morning is an excellent investment in a healthy life.

For your morning beverage, sip a few cups of green tea or water with lemon. Drink no more than two cups of coffee. Replace it with herbal teas or freshly squeezed vegetable juice.

Start your day right with a substantial breakfast. The ideal breakfast includes lean protein, fiber-rich complex carbohydrates, and some essential fatty acids. Buckwheat with ghee or coconut butter is one good example.

Lunch should also be substantial. A mixed green salad or soup is a good lunchtime appetizer and helps with portion control. This can be followed by a normal-sized entrée, which should include your favorite protein (such as poached salmon or roasted chicken), plus sautéed or grilled vegetables. When it comes to vegetables, choose a beautiful rainbow of colors. Include at least four to five colorful foods on your plate. The brighter the colors, the better. Colorful vegetables can include carrots, peppers (yellow, red, and green), broccoli, Brussels sprouts, leafy greens, beets, sweet potatoes, and asparagus. Use herbs and spices instead of salt to flavor foods. When we eat breakfast and lunch, we will be less likely to overeat later in the day.

A smart snack can help you maintain a steady blood glucose level. Sensible snacks include raw vegetables, fruit, yogurt, nuts, and seeds. Fresh raw nuts (such as almonds, brazil nuts, cashews, pecans, and walnuts) and seeds (such as flax, pumpkin, sesame, and sunflower) are good choices for healthy essential fatty acids. Don't heat hemp or flaxseed; instead, sprinkle them on food just before eating or add them to smoothies.

Dinner should be relatively light because the digestive system needs to rest while we sleep. Vegetable soup or a green salad are good choices. Avoid heavy, hard-to-digest foods for dinner, such as meat, cheese, and bread. All eating should be completed at least three hours before bedtime.

Love Your Food

*All happiness depends on a
leisurely breakfast.*
—John Gunther

When we eat whole foods, our intake is well balanced, and we tend to eat less. A diet based on fear, guilt, and deprivation can lead to binges. I choose to approach my food with love and appreciation. I've turned a dieting dilemma into my passion project of achieving a lifetime healthy eating style. I eat simply; no complicated meals for me. If I eat complexly, bloat is on the way. I keep as much healthy food as possible in my kitchen cabinets and refrigerator at all times.

I try to keep up with my nutrition and make healthy choices daily. No matter how busy my day is, I can watch what I eat. I don't eat bread every day. I avoid bread, sugar, processed food, dairy products, white flour, red meat, and pork. If I eat meat, I opt for organic.

I don't skip breakfast. I love eating a delicious and filling morning meal. My favorite breakfast is a hearty bowl of cooked buckwheat or basmati brown rice, with ghee and cinnamon on top. It could also be wild rice, oat groats, quinoa, millet, or eggs.

My afternoon snacks include seeds, nuts, and fruit or a fruit smoothie.

I try to eat lunch before 2:00 p.m. The active time for digestion is at 10:00 a.m. to 2:00 p.m., and our digestion works most efficiently at this time. It's healthy to eat most of your meals during this part of the day. Not only is what you eat important, but also when you eat it. When your digestion improves, your mood improves too.

My lunches are similar every day. I usually have a lot of vegetables, like sautéed broccoli, carrots, asparagus, or zucchini, and some fish, which is usually wild Alaskan salmon; but sometimes I have sardines, halibut, cod, sole, chicken, or lamb instead. I start with an arugula or spinach salad with olive oil, lemon juice, and some seasonings. I make sure that I eat enough food during the day.

My dinner is light and simple, around 6:00 p.m. I usually have vegetable or lentil soup or mixed green salad with a small piece of dark bread. Some days I eat less than usual; just a glass of freshly squeezed carrot and apple juice can be right for my dinner.

A twelve-hour fast works for me. By fasting for twelve hours between 6:00 p.m. and 6:00 a.m., I free my body from the burden of digestion. The body does an amazing job of detoxifying itself. Even the short fast between dinner and breakfast causes the body to go into repair mode. This fast supports the metabolism, restores energy and the body's natural balance, and normalizes weight.

Sometimes a day is busy, and I skip lunch, which I don't like doing, but it happens. Even though I feel hungry in the evening when I do this, I choose to eat something light, such as a few spoons of cooked brown rice wrapped in seaweed or steamed broccoli wrapped in seaweed, and a dash of tamari sauce. That's why I'm hungry for breakfast, which is my favorite meal of the day.

When I have fresh carrot juice during the day, I don't crave sweets. If I still want dessert, I have fresh figs, blueberries, dried apricots or dates, or nuts and seeds for a snack. I always listen to my body attentively. It guides me well.

I don't take vitamins. All vitamins are made in the laboratory by chemists. They're synthetic. I can get all the vitamins I need from my food. There's a high level of vitamin C in lemons and grapefruit. My everyday routine includes ginger tea, water, and a large glass of freshly squeezed grapefruit and lemon juice. These help me eat less, fill me up, and nourish me nicely.

When I work out in the morning, I don't eat breakfast first. I drink a healthy rice or pea protein powder smoothie afterward, with a handful of goji berries, a banana, some blueberries, flaxseed, pumpkin seeds, bee pollen, turmeric, and water. I like to personalize my smoothies and other food with different condiments, such as cinnamon, cardamom, and turmeric.

Better choices create better health. The food you choose plays a crucial role in how healthy and energetic you are. Recharge your energy wisely. Once you make some changes in nutrition, you start to enjoy natural food. As your body gets healthy, you begin to take pleasure in eating real food. You will feel better after one or two weeks of eating well nutritionally.

Comforting Soups

Try nurturing meals in the form of delicious soups. Soup can be preludes to meals, first courses, or main dishes. Soups can be eaten for breakfast, lunch, or dinner. We all need to eat a varied diet, and a pot of soup is one of the best ways to do that. In cooking comforting soups, use the best and freshest ingredients possible to stay well. The ingredients found in a vegetable-based broth are a harmonious mix of fresh vegetables, like onion, garlic, carrots, and celery; and herbs, like thyme and parsley root. Brighten your soup with herbs, spices, and fresh scallions. You can prepare homemade soups from vegetables, lentils, or meat (such as chicken or fish).

Lovely Condiments

For centuries, spices have been used to preserve food and enhance its flavor. When shopping for condiments, look for a variety of choices that can be placed within arm's reach at mealtime. If you're just beginning your collection, try including one from each of the different palate tastes: salty, sweet, spicy, sour, pungent, and nutty. Also try tamari, brown rice syrup, cayenne pepper, apple cider vinegar, garlic, turmeric, and pumpkin seeds.

Condiments create enjoyable individualized meals. Each also has a different health benefit. Create a condiment tray for your table and personalize every meal.

- Tamari: aids digestion and has less sodium than table salt or soy sauce.
- Brown rice syrup: provides a sweet taste without a rapid spike in blood sugar levels.

- Cayenne pepper: enhances blood circulation, warms the body, and stimulates digestion.
- Apple cider vinegar: cleanses the digestive tract and increases circulation.
- Garlic: stimulates the metabolism and is antibacterial and antifungal.
- Turmeric: one of many wonderful and vibrant Indian spices. It's famous for its anti-inflammatory properties and as a digestive aid.

Here are some recommended condiments worthy of experimentation. Feel free to add your favorites.

- Basic spices: cinnamon, cumin, curry powder, garlic, ginger, oregano, or turmeric
- Peppers and salts: freshly ground black pepper, cayenne, chili powder, chili flakes, or sea salt
- Vinegars: apple cider, balsamic, or red wine
- Oils: extra-virgin olive, coconut, sesame, or toasted sesame
- Sauces: Bragg's amino acids, hot sauces, salad dressings, or tamari
- Sweeteners: agave nectar, barley malt, brown rice syrup, honey, maple syrup, or stevia
- Others: ketchup, mustard, pickles, sauerkraut, or jalapeños

Spice up your meals with healing and lovely condiments. Stay healthy and vigorous.

Do you agree that the food you eat affects how you look and feel?

CHAPTER 12
_____

General Remarks about Food Combining

To wish to be well is a part
of becoming well.

—Seneca

A Well-Balanced Diet Meets Food Combining

The benefits of food combining are incredible: less abdominal bloating, less intestinal gas, the ability to drop excess weight, increased nutrient assimilation, more energy, and a lighter feeling. A well-balanced diet centered around fruits, vegetables, whole grains, nuts, legumes, healthy fats, and lean protein like fish has been shown to lead to robust health. When healthy food choices meet food combining, it creates a magic formula for wellness.

When I was searching for the quickest way to regain health and vitality, I came across very interesting information about proper food combining, a book by Peter Kelder *Ancient Secret of the Fountain of Youth*. It was a time-proven method of eating simple foods, one or two foods at a meal. I truly believe in time-proven methods. They've stood the test of time for a reason. This method of eating caught my attention because it enhanced digestion. I knew from my own experience that well-functioning digestion is necessary for good health. I made proper food combining my everyday approach to eating. It's simple, easy, and economical. I replaced my old eating habit with a new one. Proper food combining ensures better nutrition, better digestion, and more comfort.

What I learned from my research was that Tibetan monks produced their own food and ate a predominantly vegetarian diet with the addition of some eggs, butter, and cheese. The monks ate only one kind of food per meal. One food at a meal is ideal. I don't think we need to go to that extreme. They knew how to combine foods properly for better health. We can reap the fruits of their knowledge. We can combine their time-proven method with the convenience of our modern food stores and the incredible variety and abundance that are available. We can also learn to be very selective in choosing simple, natural, healthy food. We can benefit from the West and the East simultaneously.

The foundation of good health and strong immunity is in our stomach. Building a healthy digestive tract is an important step in restoring the body's balance. When we give our gut a little love and attention, it pays us back with ease and comfort. Food combining is a shortcut to better digestion.

Food Combining

Food combining is an essential part of the cleansing process and can be your daily eating routine. With improper food combining, digestion can be delayed for three to eight hours because more energy is needed for the digestive process. This creates fatigue. It can also cause depression, irritability, negativity, and cynicism. It weakens the immune system and causes premature aging. With proper food combining, the body doesn't need as much energy for digestion. As a result, you'll probably feel a noticeable increase in energy. When foods are properly combined, digestion works well, nutrients are easily absorbed, and overall health improves.

It is simple to learn which foods go well with one another. A good combination of foods is proteins (meat, including poultry and fish; dairy products, including cheese and eggs; lentils; beans; tofu; nuts; and seeds) with vegetables and healthy fats.

Another good combination of foods is starches (grains, potatoes, yams, pumpkin, corn, artichokes, coconut, sweet potatoes, beets, carrots, parsnips, and winter squash) with vegetables and healthy fats. Vegetables encourage the digestion of proteins and starches.

When you eat a variety of foods at the same meal, combining proteins with starches, as we often do (for example, chicken, vegetables, rice, and potato), this combination of foods puts a strain on the digestive process. The stomach struggles to digest this variety of foods. This usually produces gas, indigestion, bloating, and heartburn.

I divide my plate into two parts. The bigger part, about 80 percent, is for vegetables; and the smaller part, about 20 percent, is for protein and fat or starch and fat. I incorporate this technique into all my meals. It's an efficient, healthy, and low-cost diet. I just integrate simple rules of food combining into my eating routine.

Some general rules about food combining are as follows:

- Don't mix milk with meat (including fish).
- Don't eat cooked and raw foods in the same meal (raw foods are harder to digest).
- Don't eat fruit with other foods (make fruit a separate meal, snack, or dessert).
- Avoid eating leftovers or habitually eating reheated foods (freshly made foods are ideal).
- Don't drink anything while eating (drinking beverages while eating inhibits complete digestion).
- Don't eat dessert after a meal (make dessert a separate meal or snack).
- Eat only when your body is naturally hungry (stop eating when you're satisfied).
- Learn to combine foods to derive the most energy.
- Develop several recipes for healthy dishes you enjoy and can make quickly and easily.
- Don't eat when you're very emotional (angry, worried, or upset).
- Eat your food with a spirit of gratitude and love.

Within a month of proper food combining, you'll have more energy and improved digestion and metabolism, and you'll be more satisfied with your weight. You can also prevent high blood pressure, high blood sugar levels, and high cholesterol.

The right combinations of food, the right portion sizes, and the right methods of preparation produce wonderful results. My favorite part of the system is that by focusing on a good combination of foods, I get to eat what I like. This strategy works miracles.

The Seven-Day Eating Plan

The seven-day eating plan can become a healthy lifetime eating style. It can help you launch a new and healthy eating routine. Any eating plan should be individualized. Use this menu as a guideline for your own favorite foods. The following dietary schedule is beneficial and light. Remember, the purpose of these seven days is to enjoy food and improve overall health and even to lose a pound or two without food deprivation.

An everyday mantra is to eat in moderation. Sometimes, when you're less hungry, you may eat smaller portions or even eat only half the food I list for any meal (for example, eat only a salad and skip the chicken and vegetables or vice versa).

Some of us have a habit of skipping breakfast, which can lead to health consequences. Do an experiment. For two weeks, eat breakfast and track your energy level on a scale of 1 to 10 each day.

Breakfast and lunch should both be substantial and delicious.

Try to eat dinner fairly early, at least three hours before bedtime. Large dinners have a great risk of leading to excess weight. After a light dinner and a sweet and restful night, you may wake up with a ravenous appetite.

Day 1

- Breakfast: buckwheat with one tablespoon of ghee (soak the buckwheat in water for ten to fifteen minutes before cooking it).
- Lunch: mixed green salad with sliced avocado, walnuts, olive oil, and lemon juice; toast (bread should have no yeast or sugar and should be all natural); and baked or poached salmon with broccoli, peppers, Brussels sprouts, tomatoes, and asparagus.
- Snack: natural plain yogurt. Having a snack before you leave work can help you avoid mindless eating when you get home.
- Dinner: vegetable soup.

Day 2

- Breakfast: omelet with your favorite vegetables, and fresh herbs and spices.
- Lunch: mixed green salad with sliced avocado, pumpkin seeds, olive oil, and lemon; bread; and steamed trout with your favorite vegetables.
- Snack: fresh fruit salad.
- Dinner: barley soup.

Day 3

- Breakfast: brown rice with a tablespoon of ghee and a dash of cinnamon.
- Lunch: spinach salad with onion, green pepper, tomatoes, olives, cucumber, olive oil, and lemon juice; dark bread; lima bean; and vegetable soup.

- Snack: fresh fruit salad.
- Dinner: smoked salmon and vegetables wrapped in pita.

Day 4

- Breakfast: millet with ghee and cinnamon.
- Lunch: arugula salad with olive oil and lemon juice, bread, and sautéed tofu with your favorite vegetables.
- Snack: baked apple with cinnamon.
- Dinner: lentil soup.

Day 5

- Breakfast: quinoa with ghee and cinnamon.
- Lunch: mixed green salad with olive oil and lemon juice, boiled lamb, and steamed vegetables.
- Snack: freshly squeezed carrot and apple juice, or green apple and spinach juice.
- Dinner: baked sweet potato with broccoli, cauliflower, and carrots.

Day 6

- Breakfast: oats with ghee and cinnamon.
- Lunch: mixed green salad with olive oil and lemon juice, dark bread, and fish kebab with grilled vegetables.
- Snack: dried apricots or nuts.
- Dinner: toasted bread with lox, spinach, onion, and pickle.

Day 7

- Breakfast: poached egg, avocado, and roasted sea-weed snack.
- Lunch: mixed green salad, and roasted chicken with roasted vegetables.
- Snack: pineapple fruit salad.
- Dinner: broccoli soup.

You can compare your usual diet with this sample and see what works best for you. If you don't eat according to your chosen eating plan on a particular day, don't beat yourself up about it. Try again until you feel comfortable. Dietary and lifestyle changes don't happen overnight. They happen one small step at a time.

Taste of Spring

When spring comes, it's the best time to nourish and cleanse your body, burn fat, and fast. I don't usually wait for spring to get a gentle cleanse. I do it a few times a year when I feel the need to get lighter. I always turn to botan-ical medicine to encourage my body to work well. Some signs that my body needs help with gentle internal cleans-ing include low energy, weight gain, insomnia, dark under-eye circles, dull skin, poor digestion, nausea, moodiness, leg cramps, and brain fog. When I notice some of these signals, I know it's time for my gentle cleanse.

You can choose from different types of cleanses, including drinking fresh green juice, dandelion tea, and ginger tea, and watch portion size. Portion size must be adjusted to meet individual needs. You may need to eat smaller meals four to five times a day.

My detox plan includes dandelion, which is a very popular herb in three ancient herbal traditions: Western, Chinese, and Ayurvedic. It's traditionally used to support liver function. Cleansing with herbs is pleasant and effective.

Dandelion is regarded as a liver and kidney tonic in traditional medicine. It has also been used to improve digestion. Add the leaves of dandelion to your salad or brew the roots and leaves into a tea. I take a cup or two of dandelion root tea and ginger tea each day during my detox plan. I also enjoy adding dandelion leaves to green salads.

Mix in avocado, grated celery root, basil leaves, baby arugula, cucumber, and peeled tomatoes; and add your favorites.

Dandelion salad (Serves 3-4)

1 c. dandelion leaves
1 medium carrot, grated
2 c. spinach
1 small fennel bulb, thinly sliced (1/2 c.)
1/2 stalk celery, thinly sliced
1 c. chopped parsley

Dressing

2 tbsp. olive oil juice of 1/2 lemon
3 cloves garlic, pressed (2 tsp.)

Combine salad ingredients in large bowl.
Add dressing ingredients to salad. Toss
and serve immediately.

Fennel seeds can calm your stomach and prevent
unwanted gas and bloating. These tasty seeds are a good
source of fiber, vitamins, and minerals. Add one teaspoon
of fennel seeds to a cup of hot water and let it brew for five
minutes. Or try the seeds raw when you're on the go.

The quickest way to regain health and vitality is to
feed your body balanced nutrition, keep portions in check,
track what you eat, cleanse your body periodically, and
exercise regularly. We can create a menu for staying healthy
and beautiful. Now is the perfect time to eat a little cleaner
and greener.

Menu Options for a Gentle Cleanse

This menu has been adapted from *One Spirit Medicine*
by Alberto Villoldo. I tend to modify any suggestions to my
preferences. Below is my version of the detoxifying menu.
Here are some suggestions for meals and snacks.

- First breakfast of the day (7:00 a.m.): green juice
  made of six small leaves of kale, two leaves of col-
  lard greens, one cucumber, two stalks of celery,
  half inch of ginger, and one green apple.
- Throughout the day: green tea (one or two cups)
  and plenty of water, at least eight glasses, and one
  glass with the juice of half a lemon added.
- Second breakfast of the day (10:00 a.m.): protein and healthy fats of your choice—eggs, goat

cheese, avocado, smoked fish, and nuts are all great options; or one bowl of cooked whole grains, such as millet, brown rice, amaranth, quinoa, or buckwheat. Choose either protein or carbs.

- Lunch (1:00 p.m.): green salad or a serving of steamed vegetables. Eat a variety, including roots, stems, and greens of yams, green beans, broccoli, cauliflower, carrots, beets, asparagus, kale, chard, brussels sprouts, and cabbage. Use healthy oils, spices, and herbs for flavor. Combine with a handful of nuts or seeds, or an avocado, or a serving of smoked or steamed salmon, or other fish. Salmon is high in healthy oils, which are crucial to a healthy immune system. Enjoy the benefits of eating tasty fish.
- Afternoon snack (3:00–4:00 p.m.): either nuts and seeds, avocado mashed with herbs and spices, a small salad, or green juice; and one piece of fresh fruit, such as pear, apple, pineapple, or citrus.
- Dinner (try to finish by 6:00 p.m.): same as lunch. You may need to eat smaller meals four to five times a day. Try to choose either a green salad, steamed vegetables, or a small serving of fish.

Healthy methods of food preparation include grilling, steaming, boiling, and sautéing. When I cook, I always use ghee, fennel and cumin seeds, grated ginger, and turmeric.

A gentle cleanse can be accomplished with herbs by drinking a cleansing tea; by eliminating dairy, fried food, red meat, sugar, white flour products, soda, alcohol, and processed foods; and by eating light, nutritious meals for one week. This can assist the body, particularly the liver, in eliminating toxins, and replenishing and rejuvenating the blood. It's one of the fastest ways to enhance the body's healing processes.

You can also cleanse your body safely and effectively with a juicing program. Juicing is an excellent way to get desired nutrients. Begin drinking freshly squeezed vegetable and citrus juices on a regular basis. Each vegetable has the power to heal a particular organ. For instance, beets and dandelion help heal the liver. Use small amounts because they have a strong cleansing effect on the liver. Citrus fruits also support the liver-cleansing process.

Most importantly, cleanse your mind of negative thoughts. Stay focused on the positive. Aspire to perform your daily tasks in the most positive way.

I use a sauna or steam room during my cleanse. During this time, I also drink more and eat less (simple foods that digest easily).

You can create radiant health in as little as a month and maintain it all your life. Reach your absolute best in terms of your improved health and happiness. Put yourself first. You deserve to live an extraordinary life. Say yes to health and beauty.

Have you considered the benefits of food combining?

CHAPTER 13

General Remarks about a Food Journal

Health is a relationship between
you and your body.
— Terri Guillemets

Health by Your Design

What is your diet like? Does it taste good? Does it feel good? If you are like me and want to improve and create health in every way possible, there is definitely a place in your life for a food journal. My food journal was the starting point to express my thoughts about nutrition, exercise, and personality. I wanted to learn more about my nature: what I like and dislike, and what brings me comfort and discomfort. When I realized that my precious health was truly important, I decided to take action. I wanted to create radiant health by my own design and based on my unique individuality. I had a strong desire to take an active part in my wellness journey. The process of keeping a food journal was fun, informative, and even soul-searching. It was a powerful, useful, and interesting tool. It helped me improve my dietary habits and make my eating style simple, delightful, and nutritious.

I got a journal. You could also use a notepad or keep your journal on your computer. I kept a slow and steady food-combining approach to my dietary choices, making sure they fit with my broader lifestyle. I tried not to do everything at once. First, I went through my kitchen cabinets and saw what I had. Then I organized my food, and prepared to shop for missing items. Second, I planned my meals. When I went to a grocery store, I had a list of foods I needed to buy. Planning ahead allowed me to shop sensibly. I enjoyed cooking and spent more time in the kitchen. I listed my meals daily, paying attention to what I ate and how I felt physically and emotionally afterward. I learned to notice my thoughts and feelings.

For people who don't like to cook or who cook only occasionally, there is a great variety of well-prepared, delicious foods. Many stores have a prepared foods section.

I don't like wasting food. We've all been to events where piles of food get thrown away. A staggering amount of food is wasted. A staggering number of people don't have enough food. I usually take time to think about being a more conscious and less wasteful consumer (make grocery lists, plan menus, and cook fresh food daily). I choose food intelligently, based on how it can nourish and heal every cell in my body. I eat small portions with nutritional value and wonderful taste. I try to make an eating plan easy, enjoyable, affordable, and delicious.

Digestion of a meat usually takes five to six hours. That's why I try to eat meat early in the day and not every day, and eat more lightly at dinner. For dinner, which I eat about 6:00 p.m., I like vegetable soup or a salad.

Drinking herbal teas and plenty of water throughout the day, as well as freshly squeezed vegetable and citrus juices, is pleasurable.

Most importantly, sugar or sugary things should be very limited. I avoid white table salt, white sugar, and white flour. This eating plan tastes delicious and works well for me.

By starting a good relationship with my own body, I've changed my diet mentality for the better. I gradually discovered which foods were right for me. I listened closely to my body's signs and signals while trying different foods. For instance, if I got gas or heartburn after eating a certain food, I knew right away that that food wasn't for me.

Choosing healthy and tasty foods, and learning to combine them properly, was the greatest investment I could make in myself and my future health. In addition, it helped me recognize that healthy weight change is a natural result of healthy eating and living.

My best supporters of a healthy and happy lifestyle are water, sun, fresh air, herbs, balanced nutrition, exercise, yoga, meditation, massage, reflexology, acupuncture, nature walks, pleasant conversations with friends, inspirational reading, good sleep, relaxation, and a positive mental attitude, all of which my food journal helps me keep track of. Life is wonderful and includes a long list of healthy and enjoyable activities in which we can indulge.

I wrote in my food journal every day, and it became my good friend. I shared my thoughts, feelings, intentions, plans, and goals. It helped me transform my way of thinking. It helped me organize my thoughts. I could see what was going on in my life more clearly. It brought to the surface unresolved issues, hidden opportunities, and creative insights. Nutrition and mental health go hand in hand and provide healing on emotional and physical levels, which creates a holistic approach and leads to picture-perfect health. My opinion of myself also began to improve.

While I experimented with food, lifestyle, thoughts, and feelings, and celebrated each step I achieved, I could see freely what road in life to take—one that leads to a positive mindset for health and happiness. I'm still learning how to create a positive and favorable environment. It's a wonderful process of self-enrichment. By allowing myself to be in the process, surrounded by an enjoyable atmosphere of creating my best life, a spark of motivation for a healthy way of living began to form.

I appreciate that I chose an approach that fosters a mind-body connection, and I've been able to take steps toward radiant health. Keeping a food journal has been a lovely experience. It turned out to be all about my personal journey. It helped me make changes in myself and in my life easily, gradually, and creatively. I was able to make peace with food. Keeping this journal also gave me a chance to explore and improve other important aspects of life and move forward well prepared.

If you're serious about changing your diet, start with a written journal, noting everything you eat, drink, and think every day. Listen to your body. It's easy to see your habits clearly. Then you can adjust your eating and lifestyle according to your needs. You can create a lifetime eating style with the assistance of a food journal. Make your journal a healthy dose of pleasure and fun. Write down your goals and go for them. Choose to be flexible and smile often.

Mindful Eating

The pleasure of eating lies in slowing down and fully experiencing the food we eat. Time spent eating mindfully is time well invested. If you want to try a mindful approach to health, test the waters with mindful eating.

Here is a great mindful eating approach. When you pay attention to how you eat, meals become satisfying and delightful. Food must be a pleasant experience. Mindfulness in eating is about having a good relationship with food and yourself. A good relationship with food will help you gain and maintain health and an ideal weight. Mindfulness involves what you eat and how you eat. Having an occasional meal in silence and spending quality time with yourself feels marvelous.

Optimal digestion starts in the mouth. Prepare yourself to eat slowly. Eating begins with the simple art of chewing. Chewing leads to smooth digestion and greater assimilation of nutrients. Eat your delicious and nutritious meals at a table instead of the computer or TV. When you're distracted, you can easily eat too much, plus you may not even enjoy your food.

Make sure your bites are mindful. Give all your attention to your food. Look at it. Smell it. Begin to chew. Chew slowly. Each bite should be tasted. Try counting the chews in each bite, aiming for thirty to fifty times. It helps if you put your fork down between bites. Enjoy every bite. Let the simple act of chewing relax you. Taking the time to chew will help you enjoy the whole spectrum of tastes and aromas that make up the meal. It takes about twenty minutes for your stomach to tell your brain that you've eaten enough. As soon as you're satisfied, stop. When you chew your food thoroughly, digestion becomes efficient, and your body will begin to feel wonderfully light.

Search for balance between eating and physical activity. When you want to reach an ideal weight, eat more vegetables, and eat a diet that is well balanced between proteins, carbohydrates, healthy fats, vitamins, and minerals. Most importantly, send positive wishes of radiant health, energy, abundance, love, and happiness to yourself. It's a wonderful meditation with a powerful healing effect. I take pleasure in mindful eating and hope to do it more often.

I've learned to enjoy eating in silence, moment to moment. Find peace and enjoyment in mindful eating. It's an excellent investment in a healthier you.

Eating mindfully is effective and pleasurable. It's like food therapy. Create a daily retreat of eating mindfully. When you eat healthfully and chew food thoroughly, you feel fuller and satisfy your appetite with less food. Make mindful eating a conscious, self-aware choice without any judgment. Seek health, enjoyment, and pleasure in every meal of the day.

Enjoy the benefits of slowing down and savoring every bite. Live fully and mindfully in the present moment. There's magical power in the present moment. Discover your own approach to mindful eating and mindful living. The more mindfulness in our days, the better. Learning to live healthfully is practicing mindfulness. Be persistent and patient in creating your intelligent and wholesome eating style. Learn and practice the art of mindful eating.

Gourmet Buffet

Start with a mini kitchen makeover. Begin by taking a quick look through your refrigerator and get rid of items that have expired. Make some room for fresh produce. When the kitchen looks clean and inviting, it increases your enjoyment of preparing nourishing meals. Prepare food with love.

I take pleasure shopping. I go there to buy what I need for the coming week. After I'm done with my grocery shopping, I stop at a gourmet buffet, also known as a salad bar. I go through the buffet at my local supermarket and pick up freshly made food. There are many different and creatively prepared foods from which to choose. I usually opt for fish and a wide variety of vegetables and salads.

I'm grateful for the abundance in our stores and for the people who skillfully prepare the delicious foods in the salad bars.

The day I shop, I usually don't cook. I prefer to shop and eat, and to enjoy the convenience of freshly prepared foods. It's a simple way to choose what I like. Let people do what they do best: cook the perfect food. It saves me time and effort. Sometimes people say to me, I don't know what to eat. Just make a pleasant trip to a salad bar and explore.

Experiment with a variety of absolutely tasteful and appealing-looking meals. You'll definitely find food that offers healthy vibes, and it will be impossible to resist.

The kitchen is clean. The refrigerator is full of fresh produce. The menu is planned. The food from the buffet is ready. Now it's time to set the dinner table beautifully and get into a positive mood to make your mealtime joyful.

Have you tried keeping the food journal? Are you a mindful and conscious eater?

CHAPTER 14

General Remarks about Exercise

To enjoy the glow of good
health, you must exercise.
—Gene Tunney

The doctor of the Future will give no
medicine, but will involve the patient in the
proper use of food, fresh air, and exercise.
—Thomas Edison

Move Daily

A well-balanced diet goes hand in hand with physical activity. My health and beauty philosophy comprises good nutrition and adequate exercise. Physical activity is great for our muscles, bones, and brains, and is the key to achieving long-term wellness. It's essential for mind, body, and spirit to maintain balance and equilibrium.

There are many reasons to move your body daily, such as increased circulation, flexibility, and energy; improved heart health, body tone, digestion, and focus; and relieved tension.

The main goal of exercise is to encourage the flow of energy evenly throughout the body. We can recharge energy by increasing our circulation. According to Chinese medicine, all illness is a result of blocked and stagnant energy. The ancient Chinese believed that when chi, or energy, is stalled in the body, it creates imbalance, and we get sick. When chi flows freely and smoothly, the body's systems and organs are in a state of harmony and balance. Physical activity also improves the function of the skeleton, as well as of the respiratory, lymphatic, and digestive systems. It keeps us young and fills us with vitality.

Try to find an exercise style that works for you. It can be tailored to your own needs and to the amount of time you have to spend on body maintenance. Choose your favorite exercise and include it as part of your daily life. And remember, exercising too much or too little can work against you.

For people who are overweight, yoga, swimming, and other water exercise are good to begin with, but first adjust your diet. To maintain your fitness level, you should work out three to five times a week. Aim for a healthy weight and moderate physical activity of at least thirty minutes on most days. Focus on health instead of trying to lose weight. Let your body find your natural ideal weight. Your ideal weight will come to you as a reward. By making small changes consistently, pounds will come off gradually, and you'll feel lighter and healthier. Give your body one or two days per week to rest and reenergize. When you're resting, you can still do some walking.

Find a combination of good eating habits and adequate exercise. A slow but deliberate pattern of looking after your health will help make the transition easy and comfortable. Achieving a health transformation brings immense pleasure.

We can usually live on less food than we normally eat. Cut back on portions. Use a smaller plate to eat less.

What do you want to do with your body today? Find a place where you can enjoy sports or other calorie-burning activities: a gym, yoga class, dance studio, or the privacy of your own home. Or try something new. You can design a workout based on your energy level. Make a personal promise and do it. Exercise daily if possible or at least routinely.

A Happiness Walk

Many fitness alternatives are available. Walking is one of the best and most undervalued forms of exercise. Even if you don't have time to go to the gym or work out, take a long walk through a local park or get off the subway a stop early and walk home. This will get your heart pumping and provide the exercise your body needs to stay healthy.

You can start with walking and stretching, and gradually move to a more advanced body routine. Try brisk walking for twenty minutes every day or every other day. Start walking this week. Choose a pace and distance that are comfortable for you and add on to that every week. Take a pleasant walk along the ocean or in a park. Make walking a permanent part of your lifestyle. Daydream and breathe fresh air. Breath is life. Also, seeing the sky and nature is peaceful and beautiful. It balances the mind and body. A regular walking-in-the-sun routine has the bonus of filling us with vitamin D. It's the simplest and most convenient way to reach your health and fitness goals.

I indulge in a happiness walk, especially when the weather is nice. During my happiness walk, I turn my attention to breathing fresh air, exhaling tiredness, inhaling energy, and feeling the fresh flow into my lungs and cells. I talk to myself mentally: *Fresh air in, stale air out.* When I'm tired after a long and busy day, I enjoy taking my happiness walk. It calms me immediately. It works for me, and it can work for you too.

Walk, run, ride a bike, or play some tennis—move your body however you like. Regular exercise is one of the most beneficial things you can do for your blood sugar and your overall health. Plan to socialize around exercise. Meet with health-minded people for yoga class or go out dancing. Enjoy the process of becoming healthier and happier.

Perfect Posture

Good posture, stretching, and muscle tone are basic requirements for great health. Our posture plays a fundamental role in determining how we look and feel. It's the basis for a fit body. When our back is straight and correctly aligned, it looks attractive and healthy. It means we're in balance. Bad posture leads to a lack of vitality and contributes to a number of minor health complaints like headaches, poor circulation, physical and emotional tension, back pain, fatigue, and indigestion. It shows that the body is imbalanced.

By seeing yourself in a mirror, you can realize how you should stand. Your reflection reveals whether you're out of line. Without looking in the mirror, it's hard to judge whether you position and use your body to stand correctly.

Maintain your posture, and improve it no matter how old you are. My technique is simple. When I exercise, I remind myself to keep my back straight. I try to be conscious of keeping my body in the right position.

Flat Stomach

I was so inspired when I saw a beautiful woman with perfect abs on the cover of a health magazine. Immediately, my goal was to get moderate-to-vigorous aerobic exercise, which is any kind of activity, such as running, swimming, and cycling, that breaks a sweat to reduce belly fat. In addition, I could firm my arms, butt, and thighs; tone my legs; boost my metabolism; and improve my brain function. It was a win-win idea. I was aiming for at least one hour of two to three days a week of aerobic activity, such as brisk walks, step classes, or weight classes for maximum benefits.

Aging and loss of muscle mass slow the metabolism, which can play a role in increased abdominal fat. Abdominal obesity may also reflect insufficient consumption of fruit and vegetables, and lack of daily exercise. Challenge your muscles.

Consistently put your body through resistance. Imagine yourself with a beautiful tummy that is in proportion to your body type. Design a style of exercise and work toward your goal. Rewards are great, including improved physical appearance and bone density. When your stomach is firm, standing straight comes naturally.

When you want to blast off fat, flatten your stomach, have more energy, and brighten your mood, try doing some old-fashioned crunches (they work well), taking no sugar, doing proper food combining, drinking ginger tea, doing portion control, skipping dinner, drinking green juice, cleansing periodically, eating berries, and eating lots of green vegetables (they are low in calories and rich in nutrients). It takes a few weeks to see a difference. The good news is, it is possible to make and love your flat stomach. Be patient, gentle, and loving with yourself.

Stretching

Slow stretching improves flexibility and strength, and helps firm and tone the body, as well as relieve tension. Good stretching works by increasing flexibility, especially in the spine, which has connections to every part of the body. When the spine is healthy, vitality and posture improve. Gentle lengthening of the spine and muscles helps flush emotional tension and muscle tightness.

I stretch, sometimes with a yoga DVD, in the comfort of my own home. I love stretching my body in the morning and before any other exercise. It plays an important role in my exercise routine and helps me cope better with life's ups and downs. Stretching and breathing make muscles relax, improve circulation, and give pleasure. If you stretch five to seven times a week, you'll feel better and have a fitter body.

Breathing

When we breathe, especially fresh air, which is all around us, we supply our bodies' cells with oxygen. When we don't breathe well enough, our cells don't get enough oxygen and cannot function well. As a result, we feel tired.

Correct breathing techniques are the basis of many ancient healing philosophies. According to Indian philosophy, ill health is caused by an excess of mucus in the body and stale air in the lungs. Breathing is a natural therapy for healthy lungs. The lungs are responsible for filtering oxygen and delivering it to the bloodstream. We can strengthen our lungs by going for a walk in nature. Correct breathing improves circulation and helps cleanse the body and allows the body to heal. It promotes both physical and mental relaxation. Our breathing is often wrong, but we can learn to breathe properly.

There are many different breathing techniques to try, including long, deep breaths.

The most fundamental yogic breathing technique is simply long, deep breathing. It calms the mind, balances the emotions, and harmonizes body, mind, and spirit. It is used in meditation and in everyday situations when you want to be in control of your emotions or be able to think clearly or act effectively. Remember two principles. First, the slower your rate of breathing, the more control you have over your mind. Second, the mind follows the breath, and the body follows the mind.

If you want to get in touch with your breathing, here's a quiet, easy exercise to follow. Lie down faceup with your arms placed slightly away from your body, palms turned up, and legs relaxed and slightly apart. If you're sitting in a chair, keep your feet flat on the floor, shoulders relaxed, and spine straight. Close your eyes. Start inhaling and exhaling as slowly and deeply as possible through your nose.

You can use long, deep breathing as a guided meditation for many aspects of self-healing. Choose your own list of qualities to meditate on and consciously receive and accept whatever concept you choose with each inhalation. Then release, letting go of the opposite quality with each exhalation. For example, inhale (health, energy, peace, strength, and positivity) and exhale (disease, fatigue, anxiety, weakness, and negativity).

Take three to five minutes. This will help you slow down. Relax and feel great.

We should learn how to breathe correctly, from the diaphragm, which allows the free flow of energy and air throughout the body. We often use only the upper part of the lungs and neglect the lower part. As a result, our breaths are shallow, and we don't get enough oxygen. We simply need to engage the whole diaphragm.

Some other techniques to consider include tai chi, yoga, qigong, karate, and Zen meditation. These all teach correct breathing as a necessary part of practice because proper breathing focuses the power of chi. This is the same force ancient Indian Vedics called prana.

One Eastern breathing technique is called qigong. In China, thousands of people practice it daily, normally, first thing in the morning or during their lunch or teatime. When practiced regularly, it helps clear the mind, aids sleep, enhances mental agility, regulates breathing, and increases vitality.

After learning such valuable information, I became more conscious of my breathing patterns. I can practice my breathing easily, inside or outside, any time of day. My favorite place is the ocean, especially in the morning, to inhale the fresh salty air with perfect breathing from my diaphragm.

Try to take nature walks often. Morning is the best time so you can start your day filled with new energy. Walk and breathe. Fill your lungs with fresh air and healing energy.

My Story

Yoga is one of the most effective techniques for restoring the body's equilibrium. It provides a proper combination of exercise and relaxation that can help us achieve perfect balance of mind, body, and spirit, and a good attitude. Practicing yoga allows us to build a healthy body, keep it in good shape, increase vitality, and strengthen our nervous system. Yoga can be transformational.

Before choosing Kundalini, the yoga of awareness, I tried many other types of yoga. Although I enjoyed the other kinds, too, when I took my first Kundalini class, it had an immediate attraction. I think Kundalini is the most effective style of yoga. It uses a form of science that was developed thousands of years ago. Kundalini yoga was revealed to the West by Yogi Bhajan. It's a great way to recharge and heal the body quickly. It gives results in the shortest possible time. When I take a yoga class, I love experiencing stretching and breathing, challenging physical exercise, chanting mantras, meditating, and relaxing. After the class, we usually drink a delicious tea. As well, I feel calm and positive.

Practicing Kundalini yoga has enriched my life physically, mentally, and emotionally.

Yoga is a wonderful journey, and I can keep developing, learning, and enjoying. I don't see an end to it. For me, yoga is a system to understand myself better. Yoga is more than postures and breathing practices. It's also about self-care, self-love, and self-exploration, which I love. Yoga has introduced me to a new and fresh realm of learning.

By practicing yoga, I can develop better balance, posture, and health. It helps me be energetic, fresh, flexible, and creative. I feel content with myself. Yoga is a beautiful therapy. The combination of properly balanced nutrition, yoga, and happy thoughts is an excellent way to develop an enjoyable and effective personal practice and create a ritual to follow every day. Be open to the healing benefits of yoga practice. Kundalini yoga focuses on awareness and rejuvenation. Take advantage of it.

The Amazing Five Rites

I actively play a role in my precious health and always look for a simple, easy, effective way to get in shape and maintain it. I've learned to pace myself. I prefer to be kind and gentle to myself, and enjoy a chosen exercise style. No matter what my fitness goals are, I can design an exercise plan that allows me to reach them with pleasure.

Some time ago, I was introduced to a very interesting book, *Ancient Secret of the Fountain of Youth* by Peter Kelder. In this book, I found the Tibetan Rites of Rejuvenation, a series of exercises developed over centuries in the monasteries of Tibet. This is a time-proven method that has always worked for me since I discovered it. There are five simple exercises to achieve health and vitality. Any one of them alone is helpful, but all five are required for the best results. I began to perform each rite three times daily, and as I watched them start to contribute to my health, I gradually increased my repetitions until I was performing each rite twenty-one times daily. This process took me six weeks. Soon I slept better, and every morning I awoke feeling more refreshed and energetic. I found the rites a perfect mind-body discipline.

I love doing the five rites in the privacy of my own home, as well as doing aerobic exercise and weight training, and taking a Kundalini yoga class. I try to do each once a week. This exercise plan works pretty well for me. If my schedule doesn't let me go to the gym, I don't get upset, as I always have my wonderful five rites with me. Most important is to have fun and find a sense of joy while doing any exercise.

Consider the Amazing Five Rites approach to getting in shape and staying healthy and fit throughout your life. By following these simple and effective exercises, you'll improve your posture, increase your energy, relax your mind, and see a noticeable change in your body shape within a matter of weeks. They can also help you balance the flow of energy through the seven chakras (energy centers), which leads to healing and rejuvenating effects and normalizes hormonal imbalances. This is a great method for establishing correct equilibrium and releasing built-up tension, as well as rebalancing mind-body tension so we can move with grace and beauty.

The following exercise program has been adapted from *Ancient Secret of the Fountain of Youth* by Peter Kelder.

Try this technique, customize it to your particular lifestyle, and fit it into your daily routine. It has specific benefits designed to restore energy, and reshape, realign, and strengthen the body. It has a positive impact on the whole body.

Always check with your doctor before starting any physical activity.

Rite 1

Stand with your arms out to your sides and your palms down. Relax your shoulders. Turn clockwise in a complete circle. Begin slowly. Breathe normally.

To prevent dizziness, focus on a spot in front of you. Look at that spot as long as you can. After you turn away from the spot, bring your focus back to it as soon as you can.

When you're finished turning, slowly lie down. Take a few deep breaths, breathing through your nose. Relax. Wait for any dizziness to pass before doing the next rite.

If you want more challenge, turn more quickly but not so quickly that you lose your balance.

Rite 2

1. Lie faceup on a padded surface with your legs extended. Have your arms are along your sides and your palms down.

2. Inhale through your nose as you lift your head, tucking your chin. At the same time, lift both legs as close to vertical as you can.

3. While exhaling through your nose, slowly lower your head and legs.

Rite 3

1. Kneel with your legs behind you and your toes tucked. Your upper body is erect. Hold your thighs with your hands and your thumbs forward. Inhale through your nose.

2. Exhale through your nose as you slowly lower your head. Gently try to touch your chin to your chest.

3. Inhale slowly and deeply as you arch your torso back over your legs. As your spine arches, your head will follow. Bend your back gently. Don't go any further than you can control. Exhale as you return to *1*.

Rite 4

1. Sit with your spine erect, your legs extended shoulder-width apart in front of you, and your feet flexed. Have your palms on the floor beside your tushy, fingers pointing forward. Have your arms straight. Inhale.

2. Exhale as you slowly lower your chin to your chest.

3. Inhale as you lift your torso, which is supported by your arms and legs. As you lift your torso, allow your head to gently move backward.

4. Bend your knees, with your feet flat on floor. Have your arms straight. Have your chest, abdomen, and upper legs form a bridge or tabletop. Exhale as you return to *1*.

Rite 5

1. Lie facedown, with your legs extended behind you, shoulder-width apart, and your toes tucked. Put your hands under your shoulders, palms down.

2. Inhale as you push your body up and flex your feet. This resembles a push-up, except that your head goes backward.

3. Bend at the hips, bringing your body into an inverted V. Gently try to touch your chin to your chest so you can see your feet, which are flat or almost flat on the floor.

4. Exhale as you return to *2*.

Being active is good for everyone, regardless of age, strength, or flexibility. We can be fit and fabulous throughout our lives. As a bonus, physical activity can lead to a toned physique and our ideal weight. We can achieve our ideal weight without starving ourselves. We can reset our metabolism, burn fat, and retain lean muscle. Invest some time every day to exercise and love your beautiful body.

I follow my own advice, eating in moderation, exercising regularly, and thinking positively. I try to direct my attention to total health and wellness, and be win-win about the food I eat and the lifestyle I lead. My magic formula for that is to eat well, move more, and beam with positivity.

Whether you're cooking delicious meals, taking yoga classes, or reading inspirational books, you must figure yourself out—what you want to do and what your strategy is—to live your best life. The choice is always yours.

We're adults, and we take our responsibilities in our own hands. We don't like to be told what to do. If we want to harm our precious health, that's our right. One day, we will start caring about our wellness because it's the easiest way to feel good. Excellent health is always waiting for us to be considered and achieved.

Have you thought of finding a style of exercise that is both beneficial and pleasant for you?

The most important mental and physical wellness points to remember are as follows:

- Be thankful for what you have. Commit to living a life filled with joy and gratitude. View everything and everyone you meet with gratefulness.
- Spend time with people who energize you. Be positive with yourself and others. Create a positive attitude and wonderful environment around you, and enjoy the process of becoming healthier and happier every day.
- Dwell on positive, encouraging thoughts. Have positive thoughts about yourself, your health, your finances, and your future on a regular basis.
- Know that the first step to being happy is to know what makes you happy. Make a clear list of everything you want in terms of abundance, relationships, careers, and vacations. Make these your goals because they reflect what makes you feel positive. Having a dream and working toward the dream are incredible.
- One day each week, treat yourself to something special. Live each day happily focusing only on the positive. Do things that rejuvenate you.
- Think about what's good about your situation. Start expecting good things in your life. Use your energy to focus on the good all around you.
- Make it a priority to become a better you. Be your most authentic version.
- Clean your home and sort out your clutter. Beautify your home with green plants or fresh

flowers. Listen to music that you find inspirational and uplifting.

- Minimize watching the television and listening to the news.
- Eat well. Adopt a properly balanced nutrition strategy. Replace unhealthy food with healthy food.
- Include exercise as part of your daily life. Experiment with physical activity and find an exercise style that works for you
- Increase your beauty sleep. Darken your bedroom and make it free of technology and noise. Make a relaxing place to dream. When you feel better, you look better.
- Treat yourself to regular daily quiet time. Recharge yourself with meditation and prayer. Explore topics of interest.

Fortunately, there are several simple things we can do to keep our precious health in top condition. Any habit can be changed for the better with the willingness to do so. Using the information I've shared with you, take a very close look at your health and take very good care of your body-mind balance. Enjoy creating your own wellness and well-being. Love yourself and make each day exceptional.

If you consider yourself a health and wellness seeker, these remarks are for you. Introspection is appropriate for any life situation.

I don't see any boundaries between mental and physical health. There's a lot of power in understanding the beautiful and deep relationship between these two. Healing happens on the emotional and physical levels. Mindfulness is a healing treatment.

Good food is also a healing treatment. They go together hand in hand and create a holistic approach to excellent health. It's a framework for optimal wellness.

During the wonderful process of getting to know myself more deeply and making changes in myself, I grew to understand myself much better, and you can do the same for yourself.

Lifestyle changes first; then it's easier to change your diet. When we experience excellent health, we can indulge fully and joyously in the beauty of everyday life. All the energy we invest in a happy and healthy lifestyle will return to us in a better quality of life. We'll have the ability to embrace life as it is and live it happily.

When we commit to living healthfully, we benefit greatly and feel more radiant. The healthiest secret I've discovered was being grateful, giving, and positive. Every step you take, make sure it's the best step for you. It will help you beam with vitality.

Once I finished writing this book, I went outside for a walk, and I admired the swans as they swam gracefully by. I thought that to transform a life does take inner work. Life is so generous to those who trust its process. There are much better days ahead.

The Art of Getting to Know Yourself Better and Seeing Life Positively

This is a practical guide to joyful living for the most important issues of everyday life. These issues include not dwelling on the negative but focusing on the positive only, loving yourself, consistently improving your character, living mindfully, achieving mental and physical wellness, and being willing to change wishing into doing. Rely on your best true friends and supporters, and be open to learn from them.

Your best true friends and supporters include the following:

- Cultivating a positive attitude
- Developing introspection
- Gaining courage
- Being honest
- Simplifying your life
- Keeping a gratitude journal
- Forgiving the past
- Trusting the natural flow of life
- Reading inspirational books

- Fostering a sense of humor
- Practicing love and kindness
- Eating a balanced diet
- Drinking plenty of water
- Enjoying physical activity
- Breathing fresh air
- Getting adequate sleep, rest, and relaxation

My favorite friends and supporters helped me develop a better belief system, which improved my positivity, health, nutrition, exercise, goals, habits, schedules, ideas, and dreams. They guided me to the simplest and most joyful way to organize all aspects of my life, explore spirituality, commit to personal growth and well-being, and create a good environment for introspection. I take the liberty to lead you to health and wellness.

Thank you for reading the book. Did it help you in any way? What will resonate with you? After reading the book, what changes/techniques are you going to introduce to your everyday life?

Suggested Readings

I share my stories and perceptions because they may resonate with you, benefit you, and inspire you.

Here are some of my favorite resources. They contain a lot of wisdom and have helped me become a better version of myself. They have greatly assisted me in developing my philosophy of life.

Books

- *Ancient Secret of the Fountain of Youth* by Peter Kelder
- *Ask and It Is Given* by Esther and Jerry Hicks
- *Change your questions change your life:* 10 powerful tools for life and work by Marilee Adams, PhD
- *Emotional Wellness:* transforming fear, anger, and jealousy into creative energy by Osho
- *Everyday Tao:* Self-Help in the Here and Now by Leonard Willoughby
- *Foods for Health:* Choose and Use the Very Best Foods for Your family and *Our Planet* by Barton Seaver and P.K. Newby, ScD, MPH

- *Gratitude Works! A 21-Day Program for Creating Emotional Prosperity* by Robert A. Emmons
- *How to Win Friends and Influence People* by Dale Carnegie
- *Juicing for Life* by Cherie Calbom, M.S. and Maureen Keane, MS, CN
- *Kundalini Yoga: The Flow of Eternal Power*, as taught by Yogi Bhajan, PhD, by Shakti Parwha Kaur Khals
- *Living on Love: The Messenger* by Klaus J. Joehle
- *Meditation As Medicine:* Activate The Power Of Your Natural Healing Force by Dharma Singh Khalsa, MD, and Cameron Stauth
- *One Spirit Medicine* by Alberto Villoldo
- *Pharmacy for the Soul* by Osho
- *Power Juices* Super Drinks by Steve Meyerowitz
- *Rejuvenation: A Wellness Guide for Women and Men* by Horst Rechelbacher
- *Spark Joy: An Illustrated Master Class on the Art of Organizing and Tidying Up* by Marie Kondo
- *The Alchemist* by Paulo Coelho
- *The Art of Exceptional Living* by Jim Rohn
- *The Best Year of Your Life* by Debbie Ford
- *The Kybalion* by Three Initiates
- *The Life You Were Born to Live: A Guide to Finding Your Life Purpose* by Dan Millman
- *The Mediterranean Diet:* Lose Weight and Feel Great With One of the *World's Healthiest Diets!* by Marissa Cloutier, MS, RD, and Eve Adamson
- *The Monk Who Sold His Ferrari* by Robin S. Sharma

- *The Tao of Health, Sex, and Longevity* by Daniel P. Reid
- *The way of HERBS* by Michael Tierra, LAc, OMD
- *You Can Heal Your Life* by Louise Hay

Courses

- CAPP: The Certification in Applied Positive Psychology Program, from Emiliya Zhivotovskaya, New York, New York
- Philosophy Works, from the School of Practical Philosophy, New York, New York
- Green medicine; a certified training in herbalism at the New York Open Center

Schools

- The Institute for Integrative Nutrition, New York, New York
- The Open Center, New York, New York

YouTube Videos

- "The Law of Attraction" by Abraham Hicks
- "Love and Fear" by Alexander Palienko
- "Reality Transurfing" by Vadim Zeland
- "Simplify Your Life" by Dandapani

About the Author

Leona Sokolova was born and raised in Odessa, Ukraine. Odessa is a beautiful and hospitable city, an inimitable pearl on the coast of the Black Sea. It has acquired a reputation as the capital of humor. Leona moved to New York City in 2000. She feels fortunate to have lived in both of these extraordinary places.

She felt restless for most of her youth because she didn't know what she wanted to do with her life. She didn't have a strong desire or special talent or calling. Some people are lucky because they know exactly what they love doing early in their lives. Leona tried many things to learn what she liked. For example, a friend who was studying to be an artist took her to art classes, but she didn't really enjoy them. She went with another friend to acting classes, but they weren't her thing either. Of course, knowing what one doesn't like is useful too. She was asked many times what she wanted to do in life, but she always had trouble answering.

One day she wondered, "Why don't I try things I enjoy for a change?" She decided to stop following her friends and be her own leader. She wanted to learn what life was all about and to uncover the truth within. She started exploring life by signing up for college. During this journey, she'd figure out her calling or niche in life, or at least it would guide her somewhere new. Her degree in Ukraine was in civil engineering, although her hobby was always nutrition and wellness. An idea of her dream job was next to her all the time in the form of a lovely hobby, but she couldn't see it for years. She was always looking for her dream job elsewhere. She worked for different people who were sure about their dreams and gave her time and energy to fulfill their dreams. She had various jobs; some financially rewarding, others less so. All of them taught her something and contributed to her life journey.

Foreign countries attracted Leona. At first, coming to New York City was an adventure. Then she realized she wanted to stay in this gorgeous and unique city, and get acquainted with it. She began to learn more about Manhattan. It was very interesting, exciting, and challenging. She chose to find her calling in New York City, another inimitable pearl, this time on the coast of the Atlantic Ocean. She's fond of port cities.

Manhattan has both many golden opportunities and many obstacles. Going through the obstacles shaped Leona's personality, making her stronger and more experienced. She tried to always look at the bright side. She still faces challenges, but they won't stop her from following her dreams. Her main desire in coming to the US was to develop her talents to help herself and others.

Nutrition and wellness has been a hobby of Leona's for many years. Then she decided to turn her hobby into a profession that she loves. It took her a few years to thoroughly research which school she wanted to attend and to pursue her love and passion for wellness. Fortunately, she went to an excellent school, the Institute for Integrative Nutrition (IIN), and became a Certified Holistic Health Counselor (CHHC). She graduated in 2007 and began working as a health counselor. She loves encouraging people to choose radiant health.

When Leona had the brilliant idea to write a book, it was very surprising and unexpected because creative writing was never her strong suit. English was her second language, and she thought she wasn't equipped to be a writer. It would be a huge challenge, but that never stopped her before. Although she never planned to be a writer, one thing led to another. She just trusted that all her choices were right. She found some goals difficult to achieve, but there was always a way. Even though it seemed impossible, she decided to go for it because her intuition told her it was possible.

Leona had to learn about using computers, typing, researching, and writing. She had to take different courses to feel confident expressing her ideas elegantly. She took creative and business writing, and advanced English as a Second Language (ESL). All the above and much more helped her prepare to write this book. She enjoyed every minute of the wonderful process. She wrote from the heart. She feels that this book can help change people's lives for the better because it's done that for her. She also feels that if any readers want to write a book, they should pursue their dream because if she can write a book, anyone can.

After doing introspection and studying various sources and teachings, Leona has learned to persevere and be patient with herself. She's also learned to listen to her body and intuition attentively and lovingly. Most importantly, she's learned to find her unique style of enjoying and celebrating day-to-day reality, which brings her a lot of joy and fills her with the desire to share her inspiration with others. The inspiration was to do something she has a passion and love for—creating health and wellness for herself and guiding others to find radiant health and sharing with others. There is only one goal: to be happy.

CPSIA information can be obtained
at www.ICGtesting.com
Printed in the USA
BVHW061019200322
631480BV00001B/4